FAST, FURIOUS, TOMMYWOOD

From Award-Winning Journalist and Producer

TOM TEICHOLZ

FAST, FURIOUS, TOMMYWOOD

The Fifth Installment of the ***TOMMYWOOD*** Series,
a Collection of Columns and Writing on Arts and Culture

A PONDWOOD PRESS BOOK

PONDWOOD PRESS
1424 4th Street, Suite 229
Santa Monica, CA 90401

FIRST TRADE PAPERBACK EDITION

The majority of the articles in this collection first appeared in print in *The Jewish Journal of Los Angeles*, some in slightly different form and can also be found at tommywood.com.

ISBN: 978-0-9883964-9-4

Set in Minion
Printed in the United States

For Amy and Natasha

CONTENTS

INTRODUCTION

In this, Volume V of The Tommywood Collection, dubbed *Fast, Furious, Tommywood*, the topics range far and wide, and occasionally go deep, on subjects as diverse as painters Arshile Gorky and Channa Horwitz, historical figures such as Winston Churchill, and movie icons such as Elizabeth Taylor, Tony Curtis, and Stanley Kubrick. I explore the role of LA in the narrative of Post-War American Art, and discover the importance and influence of California aritst Wallace Berman. There are columns about music: from Joshua Bell, the Klezmatics, Josh Kun, Israeli rock star Rita and a performance by Mark Danielewski. Mel Gibson makes a few appearances and I get to write Nazi war criminal John Demjanjuk's just epitaph. Albert Brooks writes a novel, and there are features on playwrights Jon Robbie Baitz and the late Wendy Wasserstein. Tommywood allows me a personal moment or two, as well as the opportunity to revisit the Vienna of Gustav Klimt and Arthur Schnitzler; to solve the mystery of Detective Columbo's creator; and to make the case for Abraham Lincoln being the first Jewish President. In "Fast, Furious," Tommywood gets a little *meshuggeh.*

BAGELS, BONGOS, AND JOSH KUHN

If USC professor Josh Kun had his way, the Jewish people might not be known as "the People of the Book" but rather "the People of the Record."

Jews on Vinyl, curated by Kun and Roger Bennett, of the Charles and Andrea Bronfman Foundation, is the new exhibition at the Skirball Cultural Center, where you can seat yourself on a midcentury-modern couch and tap your feet to Irving Fields' 1959 recording "Bagels and Bongos"; grin while listening to a wide spectrum of albums—from Herbie Mann's "Push Push" to Barbra Streisand's "Superman"; comedy albums by Sophie Tucker, Myron Cohen and Lenny Bruce; Leo Fuchs' "Shalom Pardner"; or even the Barry Sisters singing their Yiddish rendition of "My Way."

The exhibition, which ran in San Francisco for almost a year, is based on Kun and Bennett's 2008 book *And You Shall Know Us by the Trail of Our Vinyl* (Crown Publishing).

"When most people think of Jewish music in America, there are some very specific things they think about," said Kun, a founding member of the Idelsohn Society for Musical Preservation, alluding to cantorial and klezmer music, which he deemed hugely important. "But, that is a small slice of the Jewish musical story in the United States," he added.

In curating *Vinyl* and the upcoming Idelsohn release "Black Sabbath," an anthology of black artists singing songs that are explicitly Jewish, and which attempts to "understand Jewish music as a resource for blackness," or a planned collection of "Hava Nagila" covers, Kun, thirty-eight, is pursuing his passion—investigating music at the intersection of race, identity and popular culture.

"Our conversations [at Idelsohn] do not revolve around irony and kitsch value," Kun said recently. "They revolve one hundred percent [around] love and a deep, manic, hungry curiosity for more knowledge about what we don't know."

Kun grew up in West Los Angeles in what he describes as "a very music-loving household—not music playing but music listening." His father was a big fan of folk music, particularly of The Weavers (featuring Pete Seeger). From The Weavers, Kun learned that "music was always internationalist, came in all sorts of different languages. It was inherently political, and it was about history and community, and it was about a way of thinking about life and society."

As a high school student at the private Harvard School (prior to its merger with Westlake), Kun started writing a music column—and has pretty much been doing so ever since.

"Music was always the way I experienced things. [It is] the first thing I go to, to figure things out, to figure myself out, to figure out the world, to interact with history."

Kun went to Duke University as an undergraduate, and then to University of California, Berkeley, where he earned his doctorate in ethnic studies. He was inspired by the writings of Greil Marcus ("Mystery Train," "Lipstick Traces") to "look really hard at the relationship between American identity and music and questions of race and ethic identity."

In his thesis, which became his first book, "Audiotopia" (University of California Press), Kun took up, as he put it, "Walt Whitman's call of 'I hear America singing' to ask, 'What is America singing?' and 'Who's listening?' and 'What are the voices being heard and talked about?' "

One night, while watching *The Tonight Show,* host Jay Leno introduced the African American jazz artist Don Byron, who played music by Mickey Katz. Afterward, Leno referred to Katz's music, Kun recalls, as "bar mitzvah music," but Byron insisted it was "radical ethnic music." That Byron knew this music and saw it as radical, and Kun did not, started Kun on a journey of exploration.

Kun eventually got to know Katz's widow and sons, Ronald Katz and Joel Grey (yes, the actor). He was responsible for republishing Katz's autobiography and began to give lectures on Katz and his music. It was Kun's gateway into Jewish music.

At the same time, Kun's thesis adviser, Waldo Martin, pushed him to "take seriously the role of Jews in the drama of American race and music" and to include Katz in his dissertation, which, until then, had been primarily devoted to black and Latino issues. More importantly, Martin also urged Kun to consider his own "positionality as a white Jew writing about this stuff."

He discovered artists such as The Barton Brothers (vaudevillians who mixed Yiddish comedy and edgy klezmer), Menashe Skolnick (once called the great-grandfather of all Catskills comics) and "godfadduh" of Jewish parody Allan Sherman. He haunted the record bins, looking in "the dreaded Judaica" sections. He helped the Magnes Museum in Berkeley organize and digitize its large collection of Jewish music.

"Shalom," The Barry Sisters, Roulette, 1962 Courtesy of Josh Kun and Roger Bennett

As Kun dug deeper into Jewish recordings, he was surprised to find "all this Latin music." He started collecting Latin Jewish recordings, primarily but not exclusively New York-based Jewish-Latin exchanges from the 1930s through the 1960s. "That became my hunt."

How did Latin and Jewish music cross-pollinate? There are several theories. One has to do with Sephardic heritage, Latin by definition. Another has to do with what musician Steve Bernstein has called "the Gulf Coast theory," concerning the Jewish retirement disapora and the similarities of the rhythmic signatures between the horah and Latin music.

Kun, for his part, believes that "it's really about population contact and culture." Or, as he put it, "We have to look at the ways that Jews and Latinos were bumping up against each other, both speaking English and non-English languages, and both making music inspired by the mainstream and outside of it." For this you would have to look to East Harlem, both Spanish Harlem and Jewish Harlem and, of course, to the Catskills, where mambo mania took hold—refusing to put Jewish music—or Baby—in a corner!

"One of the stories," Kun said, "is that the guys who would buy the liquor [for the Catskills Jewish resorts] would go to Cuba and Puerto Rico, and they would hear all this [Latin] music and say, 'We've got to bring this back.'"

Kun was not alone in his enthusiasm for these hybrid music discoveries. "I met three wonderful guys: Roger Bennett, David Katznelson [of Birdman Records, among many other music labels and projects], and Courtney Holt [president of MySpace

Music]. "When we met, we bonded over our love of music and our interest in rethinking Jewish American music."

The Rosetta Stone was the discovery of Fields' *Bagels and Bongos,* a collection of mambo tunes based on Yiddish classics—or, as Bennett and Kun call it, "The White Album of the Jewish Latin Craze."

In 2005, they formed Reboot Stereophonic, a record label to reissue records they thought were important, many of which were forgotten or had never been released on CD. Over the last few years, they issued several genre-expanding recordings, from "Jewface," an anthology of transgressive vaudeville songs about Jews, to Gershon Kingsley's "God Is a Moog," a collection of Jewish liturgical Moog experiments, to Fred Katz's Buddhist/kabbalist "Folk Songs for Far Out Folk."

However, as the music industry began to change over the last few years, they decided they didn't want to be a record label. They decided to re-form as the Idelsohn Society for Musical Preservation (named for Abraham Zevi Idelsohn, the legendary musicologist and writer of "Hava Nagila"). Which means that they will still put out records but will also be "a digital site that can function as the hub for Jewish archival musical thinking," as well as a place for archives to find new audiences; a revamped Web site is planned to launch later this year.

The publication of *And You Shall Know Us by the Trail of Our Vinyl* can be seen as a manifesto for the breadth of Jewish music that Kun and the Idelsohn Society are trying to preserve: cantorial albums; Yiddish songs; comedy albums in English, Yiddish and Yinglish; Mickey Katz; records about the Holocaust, the struggle to free Soviet Jews; even Israeli disco fever. It is a declaration of all the ways in which Jews contributed to and sought to become part of the American melting pot—a conversation about the places where cultures clashed and melded. It is also plea to mail in your own cherished, eccentric and "lost" albums to be rediscovered and reclaimed. As the Idelsohn Society is wont to proclaim, "History sounds different when you listen to it."

Last summer, Idelsohn staged a live Latin Jewish music event outdoors at Lincoln Center in New York that attracted a large and diverse crowd—the old and the young, Jew and non-Jew, a veritable cross section of ages, ethnic backgrounds and sensibilities.

In the same vein, this summer, the Skirball Cultural Center, along with the Idelsohn Society, will stage a "Jews on Vinyl" live event Aug. 19.

Until then, you can go to the Skirball and enjoy a freilach cha-cha. And if you see Kun or Bennett, quote Juan Calle and His Latin Lantzmen: "Mazel Tov, Mis Amigos."

May 11, 2010

ARSHILE GORKY, KINDRED SPIRIT

Not long ago, someone brought up the painter Arshile Gorky (1904-1948) and I realized I'd always assumed he was Jewish. I was wrong; he was an Armenian Christian. But my mistake piqued my curiosity: Why did I think so? What element of his life and work spoke to me so deeply that I felt such a kinship?

I have been thinking about Gorky now because this summer, the Museum of Contemporary Art (MOCA) at Grand Avenue will present a retrospective of the artist's work. The show, which opens June 6 and continues through September 20, will consider the artist's full life's work. It was curated by the Philadelphia Museum of Art and was recently at the Tate Modern in London.

Here are some details of Gorky's life that may have led me astray:

1. He was a witness to genocide.

Gorky was born Vosdanig Adoian around 1904 (there is some confusion about the actual date) in the village Khorkom, near Lake Van in Turkey. In 1915, Turkish troops began a pogrom of murder and forced deportations of Armenians in the community, an act of systematic and thorough ethnic cleansing that became known as "The Great Crime"—for which the term genocide was coined. Turkey still refuses to acknowledge the genocide, and the issue continues to fester. Gorky and his family were among thousands who fled to the border, and, during the winter, his mother died of starvation. In 1920, Gorky and his sister immigrated to the United States.

2. He arrived in the United States at Ellis Island, changed his name and eventually settled in New York City.

In choosing the name Arshile Gorky, he claimed to be related to the Russian author Maxim Gorky. After spending some time in Massachusetts, he settled in New York.

3. He was largely self-taught and self-invented.

Much like the Jewish pioneers of the entertainment business, Gorky taught himself to be an artist. He did so by intensive study of the works of Cezanne, Picasso, Léger and Miro. During the 1930s, he worked for the WPA and painted large-scale murals for the administration building at the Newark, NJ, airport.

4. He hung out with other refugee artists.

Gorky's friends included many of the European artists that fled the Nazis for New York, including the Surrealists André Breton and Roberto Matta, but also the young Willem de Kooning, a future Abstract Expressionist.

5. He was Mark Rothko's teacher.

Gorky taught at the Grand Central School of Art in New York, where Rothko (who was indeed Jewish) was one of his students.

6. One of his paintings is called *Agony.* Need I say more?

The above may seem a somewhat glib rendering of Gorky's biography, but it reveals a certain intangible element of dislocation and longing that infuses much of Gorky's best-loved work, and that is a familiar character among Diaspora Jews.

The Gorky retrospective includes paintings, drawings and prints, and delivers a far-reaching and detailed survey of Gorky's work. As MOCA Chief Curator Paul Schimmel noted in the exhibition's press release,

"Gorky courageously reshaped European Modernism into the foundations of abstract expressionism. He inspired a generation of artists that the act of painting alone was enough to be both poetically charged and powerfully tragic."

The show allows us to witness the full evolution of Gorky's work, as well as his emotional currents. It is easy to see the influence of his masters, Picasso and Léger, and even his contemporaries, such as Stuart Davis, as Gorky develops his own vocabulary.

Many stunning canvases and drawings are included, from an early iconic self-portrait with the artist's mother, to a later work on paper, a study for perhaps his best-known work, *The Liver Is the Cock's Comb* (a work in the Surrealist style, with a Surrealist title, if ever there was one).

Gorky's exposure to the Surrealists pushed him to explore his subconscious. Even his quasi-abstract works speak to us in a language that, albeit foreign, we can understand instinctually. These works include *Betrothal I* (1947) (from MOCA's collection), in which anthropomorphic forms seem to dance before us, and *Dark Green Painting* (Philadelphia Museum of Art), one of his last works, which seems to express enormous psychic pain and foreshadows his eventual suicide in 1948.

Throughout the run of the exhibition, many programs will offer opportunities to get to know Gorky better, including Michael Taylor, exhibition curator from the Philadelphia Museum of Art, speaking about Gorky's relation to Abstract Expressionism (June 6); Richard Hovannisian, professor of Armenian and Near Eastern History at UCLA, who will speak about Gorky's Armenian heritage (June 20); and filmmaker Atom Egoyan, who will screen his film *Ararat,* in which Gorky appears as a character, at the Pacific Design Center (June 27).

Yes, Gorky was an Armenian Christian. Yet because his work speaks so clearly of dislocation, invention and reinvention, as well as of assimilating the ways of others in order to find one's own new identity, his story is our story. If Gorky seems like one of us, it is because he was. He just wasn't Jewish.

June 1, 2010

COULD *SONS OF TUCSON* BE A CULT HIT?

Sons of Tucson is a clever and subversive new sitcom about three sons who've fled to Tucson, Arizona, because their father was imprisoned for financial fraud. They then go on to recruit a ne'er-do-well, played by Taylor Labine (of *Reaper* fame), to pose as their father for school and other official purposes. The show is generating some drama of its own.

Fox, which bought the comedy to help revive its sitcom fortunes—dormant since *Malcom in the Middle* ended—originally planned to air the show on Sunday nights at 8:30. Audience testing reportedly indicated that the show would fare better at a more family-friendly time so, of course, Fox decided to air it even later on Sunday. Predictably, the show did poorly at 9:30 p.m., and, after four episodes, Fox put the show on hiatus.

Sons of Tucson returned last week, this time on Sundays at 7:30 p.m., a (somewhat) better time slot. Given this reprieve, and with support and goodwill, the show still has some chance at a second season. Justin Berfield (formerly an actor on *Malcolm*) has tweeted that he will donate half his producing fee to charity if the show is renewed. I won't ask for or make a cash contribution, but I'll do my part with a plea to watch the show—it's twisted and weird in surprising and enjoyable ways.

My own track record of picking sitcom winners has been rather uneven in recent seasons. I was a big fan of *Better Off Ted,* a wonderfully edgy corporate satire that never gained much traction; currently, I sing the praises of *The Middle,* which I find to be a contemporary *Roseanne,* one of the best-written, most affecting, most real comedies, but which is known mostly as the lead-in to the gimmicky and much buzzed about *Modern Family.*

So, what is it I like so much about *Sons of Tucson*? Why do I think that, like *Freaks and Geeks,* to which it owes a debt of inspiration, it will develop a cult following for successive waves of viewers? In full disclosure, it could be a matter of bias, as Harvey Myman, my brother-in-law, is one of the producers. But I'd prefer to believe it's my fascination with the fact that almost every character on the show is, in one way or another, a liar, hiding secrets and a fair amount of rage very near the surface, and that in spite of this, or because of this, they find themselves becoming a family—even as they are lying about being one. That appeals to me.

"There is a lot of humor that lies in people not telling the truth," show co-creator Greg Bratman told me recently.

Or maybe I was just impressed by Bratman, a first-time TV writer who sold the pilot on spec with his partner, Tommy Dewey (also known as an actor, most recently in the Zac Efron vehicle *17 Again*)—something that almost never happens.

Bratman grew up in Palo Alto (where his father is a Stanford University philosophy professor), majored in philosophy at Princeton and performed in Quipfire, the college improv troupe. After college, he plunged into acting in the New York theater scene, working with the New York Theatre Workshop and playwright Moises Kaufman, and landing a small part in the 2001 Shakespeare in the Park "Measure for Measure," alongside Billy Crudup and Sanaa Lathan. He pursued his love of improv at the Upright Citizens Brigade in New York, and, with his Palo Alto homeboy Dusty Brown, Bratman wrote and performed in *The Barrel Brothers,* the adventures of a *Flight of the Conchords/ Smothers Brothers*-esque folk duo from Kansas.

While in New York, Bratman also connected with Tommy Dewey, another alum of Princeton and Quipfire. They started to write together, creating two-man shows, including *Natalie,* a play for eight characters (in which Dewey and Bratman played four each). They presented *Natalie* at the 2003 New York Fringe Festival and then brought it to Los Angeles.

Subsequently, Dewey got cast in a number of WB programs, such as *What I Like About You* and the short-lived *The Mountain,* and Bratman and Dewey decided to try their hands at writing for TV. Somewhere in that process, they met Myman, who mentored them through a few first attempts.

In 2007, Bratman and Dewey pitched the basic idea of *Sons of Tucson* to Myman (who by then was working at J2 Pictures, the production company of Berfield and Jason Felts)—and Myman encouraged them to write it.

The concept was informed by Bratman and Dewey's experiences sitting in a New York coffee shop and listening to twelve-year-olds on cell phones bossing around their parents. Dewey was single, and Bratman didn't have kids yet (he now has a one-year-old), and they were amazed at how these kids had no boundaries. "It was hilarious," Bratman recalled.

The result is a story about kids operating without parents in a world that requires at least one, and then discovering how much they need family. Fox bought the pilot, and 20th Century Fox Television got involved. J2 Pictures recruited director Todd Holland of *Malcolm* fame as part of the creative team and to direct the pilot. As a neophyte, Bratman was grateful to be involved at every step, including casting and editing the pilot; Matthew Carlson, a veteran TV writer, came aboard as executive producer.

Thus far, *Sons of Tucson* has managed to be funny, at times sweet and often weird. True to the writers' original invention, everyone seems to be lying about something—for pragmatic rather than altruistic reasons. Yet—and this is what makes the show worth watching—you never know which way their weirdness is going to turn, despite the best of intentions.

As if writing a TV show were no small accomplishment, Bratman is also a doctoral candidate at Stanford in environmental studies. Surprising, right? A few years ago, while Dewey was pursuing acting, Bratman found himself under a four-month enforced vow of silence to repair vocal nodes damaged while performing as the Barrel Brothers. Having that much time to think had an impact. "I refocused," he said.

"If all you are doing is trying to promote yourself as an actor and writer," Bratman said, "you're at risk of going into full ego mode." He decided he needed "something bigger than myself."

What he did was get a master's degree in environmental science at UC Santa Barbara, studying eco services systems—which, in case you were wondering, are the services nature provides for humans, such as water purification, pollination or dam control—that are rarely valued. He was subsequently accepted at Stanford, and he is supposed to begin there next September.

Sons of Tucson will air its remaining episodes over the next two months—I have seen some of the upcoming episodes, including a funny and touching "Father's Day." The show's immediate fate is uncertain, but see if you don't think its future as a cult classic is assured. As for Bratman, when I asked him whether next fall would find him in Hollywood or in class at Stanford, he answered:

"I'll have to see where life takes me."

I'll be watching with interest.

June 15, 2010

BELL'S ARTISTRY RINGS OUT

Recently I sat down with violinist Joshua Bell to talk about being a classical music performer in the twenty-first century and a star in the age of iPods and auto-tuned performances. Bell, who will perform July 15 at the Hollywood Bowl, talked about how technology can enhance the concert experience, what makes for a great performer and his deepening connection to Israel.

Now forty-two, Bell has been playing violin since he was 5. He first performed in public at seven, made his debut with the Philadelphia Orchestra at fourteen and first appeared at the Bowl at seventeen, performing Tchaikovsky's violin concerto. He has appeared at the Bowl since then, by his own reckoning, "maybe fifteen times."

"There's nothing like it anywhere," Bell said of the Bowl. "There's something thrilling about playing for 15,000 people." The acoustics have improved since the recent renovation, he added, and the giant video screens "make people feel like they're closer to the action."

Bell will perform Max Bruch's *Scottish Fantasy,* completed in 1880, a work that is not as popular today as the composer's violin concerto but that in its day was, as Bell put it, a "war-horse" that Bell listened to as a child. Bell's hero, the violinist Jascha Heifetz, chose the work for his final concert, and Bell characterized the music as "a very emotional, very melodic piece," with "orchestra colors unusual for a violin concerto." Being half-Scottish, on his father's side, and Jewish on his mother's, Bell joked that the work "brings everything together."

Although not raised in a religious household, Bell explained that he has a strong connection to Israel. First of all, the violin he plays, a 1713 Stradivarius, is called the Huberman violin, because it was once owned by Bronislaw Huberman, founder of the Israel Philharmonic. That alone garners Bell respect in Israel.

Bell also recently discovered a deeper family connection to the Jewish state. Researchers working on a documentary about Huberman discovered that Bell's great-grandfather, Shlomo Avigdor (1866-1917), who came to Palestine on the first aliyah in 1891, was buried in Israel, and in May, when Bell performed in Israel, he went for the first time to visit the grave. He was struck by the fact that Avigdor was one of the first pioneers and settlers of the city of Hadera—a piece of Bell's family history that even his mother was not familiar with, as his great-grandfather had died young. Bell was also moved by seeing inscriptions on the grave that indicated that Avigdor was a cantor.

I asked Bell, who prior to acquiring the Huberman played another Strad, what makes this one so desirable. He compared the feeling for his instrument to the way a person falls in love with his or her mate instead of someone else.

"I fell in love with my violin," he said, and "within minutes [of playing it], I knew I had to have it. The very same night I tried it, I played at Royal Albert Hall for 8,000 people on the new violin, which is unusual, because it usually takes months to feel comfortable [with a new instrument]. I felt that I didn't want to play on anything else."

Bell confessed he has had his ups and downs with his violin—as one does in any relationship—explaining that there are times when he feels he has explored all he can with the instrument, and then others when he falls in love again.

"It's an ongoing discovery with an instrument like that," Bell said. "No question that I'm still finding ways of playing and ways of getting colors and sound that I didn't realize I could do—it's still happening."

I asked Bell if he's had his eye on any other Stradivariuses. He smiled, saying that he'd had his eye on one, and that if it ever became available…

As for what makes a great performer, Bell said: "The emotion in the music is everything. I don't think a performer who's just technically proficient is going to go very far, unless they're eight years old, and then they can get away with it just because it's amazing to see. Even Paganini, who was known for his technical prowess, also made women faint and people cry…There are just some people that have this personality that somehow connects with people. I really can't explain why some people can get up in front of [an audience and] make you want to watch—and you're riveted."

As he spoke, I felt he might almost have been talking about his own popularity. But, for the rest of us, it is his willingness to access his emotions on stage and let them speak through his violin—to be both conduit and performer, to stand in the present and in league with the past—that makes his appeal so tangible.

Find out for yourself July 15 at the Hollywood Bowl.

June 29, 2010

WHAT WE SAY WHEN WE TALK ABOUT MEL GIBSON

The recent news that Mel Gibson is no longer a client of William Morris Endeavor should come as no surprise. Many news and entertainment programs, including NBC's *Today Show,* pegged the delisting to Gibson's recent domestic assault allegations and tabloid leak of surreptitious tapes of racist rants he allegedly made, all arising from his custody dispute with his baby-mama Oksana Grigorieva.

But Gibson was already on borrowed time at the agency. In 2006, following his Malibu arrest and anti-Semitic rant, Ari Emanuel, then at Endeavor, writing in the Huffington Post, called on all Hollywood to shun Gibson. Gibson's great defender was his longtime agent Ed Limato, then at ICM, who famously threw a drink in the face of Page Six's Richard Johnson for comments about Gibson at a Vanity Fair Oscar party. Subsequently, Limato moved his operations from ICM to William Morris, and when William Morris and Endeavor merged last year, Emanuel and Limato found themselves having to make a cold peace.

A few weeks ago, Limato died. Then the other shoe dropped. Regarding Gibson, no one could call Emanuel a hypocrite.

For his part, Gibson's self-destructive self-immolation has cost him his marriage, much of his fortune, his standing in Hollywood and—depending on what happens next—could lead to criminal prosecution for domestic violence.

Which begs the question: Are the travails of Mel Gibson a fitting comeuppance, a vindication of those who saw something noxious in Gibson's *The Passion of the Christ,* a Shakespearean tragedy where character is destiny, or, perhaps in and of itself, proof that God exists? Or some combination of the above?

Rewinding through Gibson's oeuvre and focusing on *Braveheart, The Man Without a Face* and then *The Passion,* the consistent theme appears to be that violence and harsh confrontation beget redemption.

Gibson entered the fray with his *The Passion of the Christ.* I would argue that each generation gets the version of Christ it deserves. So, if *The Greatest Story Ever Told* was made for the post-World War II *Greatest Generation, Godspell* for the sixties flower children, and *Jesus Christ Superstar* for the "me" decade 1970s, then *The Passion of the Christ* embodies a rift in American culture, a moment when war and existential threats seemed everyday experiences. When Gibson told us he was being true to the Gospels in making his movie, he was not wrong. But it was his specific choices from among the versions that reflected Gibson's own soul and character.

The enormous success of the film is history now, but it's almost hard to remember the time when Jews questioning Gibson's *Passion* were made to seem as if they were asking for a revisionist Jewish version of the New Testament. Indeed, even Gibson's Jewish publicist, Alan Nierob, defended him.

At one point, Gibson claimed he was going to make a film about the Maccabees, which some took as a form of atonement, but which, to me, carried an implied threat—of exposing an ugly side to Jewish heroism. For most children, the Maccabees are the heroes of the Chanukah saga, but in a Gibson world of violence and martyrdom, the Judean fighters might seem closer to the Taliban, fighting against the corrupting Hellenism of their time by murdering fellow Jews.

Then, in 2006, after being arrested for driving while intoxicated, Gibson made his comments about the Jews causing all the world's wars. Privately, it seemed a confirmation of Gibson's darkest thoughts, but publicly many excused Gibson's rant as a drunkard's heat-seeking attempt to provoke with the most offensive comment possible. Gibson slipped back under the radar.

What has complicated the discussion about Gibson was that most American Jews of recent vintage spend a good deal of time hearing about anti-Semitism (and donating money to fight it), but few actually have experienced it.

I have met several Holocaust deniers and, strangely enough, I met most of them in Jerusalem—during the course of covering the Demjanjuk war crimes trial. They were always ruddy, Middle America types or English academic types. All very friendly. What they had in common was that they saw themselves as men (and they were all men) of principle committed to finding the truth. Their quibbles were obsessive: If one fact was wrong, then that proved that all the facts of the Holocaust had been false or exaggerated.

Gibson, too, seems to alternate between Mel the Gregarious and Mel the Scary, a man seeking things his way and a man out of control—with anger and self-righteousness fueling a bigotry he won't acknowledge.

For several years, Gibson seemed a time bomb waiting to explode. There was the church he funded in Malibu that didn't accept Vatican II, and then the rumors that he had a girlfriend, followed by denials, then his wife filing for divorce, and the announcement that not only did Gibson have a girlfriend, but she was pregnant with what would be Gibson's eighth child.

Did Gibson think being famous, being wealthy, put him in control? I'm sure he was warned. But an affair and a child with a much younger woman? What did he think would happen?

Which brings me back to my original question: What can we say about Gibson? There is no question that he alone is the engine of his current problems. It is also clear that his bigotry and sexism are part of his vile arsenal, and he can no longer deny the taint on his character. In the days and weeks to come, we may hear explanations for Gibson's behavior or promises of treatment of one kind or another. He may go on to make other movies, self-financed or even studio distributed (and they could even be good), but no one will ever look at him the same way again. Gibson may pray for things to work out or for forgiveness from family, friends and colleagues; and others may pray for him. But I won't be one of them.

July 13, 2010

TEN YEARS AFTER

It's been ten years since my mother died on September 22—nine since I stood by her graveside at the unveiling. Since then, I have visited her grave in New Jersey on many occasions and have diligently observed days of mourning and lit memorial candles.

I loved her dearly. But have I missed her? The answer is, of course, yes. But death does strange things: it restores our loved ones to their best selves—as we would most like to remember them—before the ravages of disease or age fully took their toll.

So I have spent the last ten years forgetting the more than twenty years before that during which my mother suffered from severe recurring depression, her multiple suicide attempts, hospitalizations, outpatient ECT treatments, her cycle of dazed, better, fine, too good, bitter, worse, bad, crazy, immobilized and unwilling, and needing to go to the hospital. Even writing this paragraph causes tension to course through me in a way that I had almost forgotten.

Since her death, my mother's smile is with me. Her wicked sense of humor, dark and cutting as it was, which in later years could turn just mean, is once again clever, witty, even insightful.

My mother had a love of culture, high and low. She had a better understanding of Shakespeare than any of my teachers ever did, but she also delighted in gossip, tabloid papers and, increasingly over the years, TV shows. How often we discussed what was on TV that night, what old movies there were to enjoy, what new sitcoms delighted, what shows in rerun she relished.

So I miss her when I watch a sitcom, or a particularly good mystery. Sometimes I'll be watching something old-fashioned, say a Masterpiece Theatre Hercule Poirot, and I will savor each detail, knowing that no one would have found it more delicious than my mother. Sometimes on the weekend, I'll turn on the classic movie channel and indulge in a communion we would have shared.

My mother was also quite glamorous. In Budapest, in her youth, my mother was what today we would call an M/A/W (model/actress/whatever) with the stage name Eva Somogyi. She cared little for her career, enjoying it as much for the social mobility it provided as the income. Since her death, with benefit of the Internet, I've been to accumulate, scan and retrieve images of her from those days. She was indeed beautiful. I have seen two of the three films that she appeared in, and I agree with her assessment that she "was not a great actress, but was cute on screen."

As I came to know her, my mother was vain, narcissistic, critical and demanding. Looks: Hers, mine, other people's—all mattered to her. The way a person was dressed, the way a table was set, manners, the paintings in a person's home, the cups that the coffee were served in at a home or a restaurant (she was against coffee served in paper cups)—nothing went unnoticed.

I miss neither the scrutiny nor the weight of such constant judgments. But I do cherish my mother's appreciation for the good, the worthy and the beautiful in all things. I often find my head filled with arcane knowledge she instilled in me about subjects—artists, dancers, long-forgotten European writers; or in thrall about movies, art exhibits or cultural events that few others seem interested in—and I miss being able to share or tell her about them. Less and less, there seem to be people I know who care as much about the things she cared about.

Just the other day, while my wife and daughter were away, I brought home dinner. I placed the takeout containers on the dining table—and stared at them. Although plastic utensils were provided and the containers were made so that I could eat right out of them, I couldn't bring myself to do so. I set the table using the best of our dishwasher-safe plates, placed the silverware with the fork laid upon the cloth napkin, placed the glass in front and served myself dinner, placing the containers away on the counter. Did the food taste better that way? I can't say. Did I appreciate it more? Perhaps. But did doing so make me think of my mother? Certainly.

September 28, 2010

THE MAN WHO WAS TONY CURTIS

Tony Curtis was so famous, so iconic an American movie star that I don't really need to tell you who he was. He was Tony Curtis, and he lived that role with childish delight, relishing where his life had taken him, and the pleasures and opportunities fame had afforded him. By the time he died last week at age eighty-five at his home in the Las Vegas suburb of Henderson, Nevada, he was known the world over—for the movies he starred in, such as *Some Like It Hot* and *Sweet Smell of Success,* for the women he loved (Janet Leigh, Marilyn Monroe), for being the father of Jamie Lee Curtis and for being a movie star from a time when being one mattered.

Curtis was born Bernard Schwartz in the Bronx. His parents were Hungarian immigrants who came to the United States following World War I. His father, Emanuel Schwartz, was a tailor who could barely support the family. His mother, Helen, suffered from schizophrenia, as did his younger brother Robert. At one point, when his parents could not support the family, Curtis and his other brother, Julius, were sent to a state institution. After the brothers returned to the Bronx, Julius was killed by a truck and Curtis fought in a street gang and endured anti-Semitic attacks.

Curtis joined the Navy in 1944, serving during World War II. Upon his return, he took acting classes on the GI Bill and was discovered by a Universal Studios talent scout. What Hollywood had to offer—girls and money, in that order—was irresistible.

It was Curtis' combination of toughness and vulnerability—his predatory sexual magnetism and the almost female quality to his beauty—that would make his career. Billy Wilder had the genius to lampoon and showcase all these contradictions in *Some Like It Hot,* casting Curtis as a jazz performer who was a womanizer and a con man who had to disguise himself both as a woman and as a Cary Grant-flavored fop. Burt Lancaster seized on Curtis' charisma and his ambition by playing opposite him in *Trapeze* and *Sweet Smell of Success.*

Once Curtis achieved success, the roles were many, but his great performances were few and far between. Although he could surprise in such roles as *The Boston Strangler* (1968) and *Lepke* (1975), more often than not he was in such popcorn fare as *The Great Impostor* (1961) and *The Great Race* (1965). Curtis also starred in the TV series *The Persuaders!* with Roger Moore for two seasons (1971-72), and later played a recurring character in *Vega$* (1978-1981). Nevertheless, over the years the role he came to inhabit best was that of Tony Curtis.

Curtis was married six times: to Janet Leigh (daughters Jamie Lee and Kelly), Christine Kaufmann (daughters Alexandra and Allegra), Leslie Allen (sons Nick and Benjamin), Andrea Savio, Lisa Deutsch and Jill Vandenberg. He did two stints at the Betty Ford Center for drug and alcohol abuse. Yet, despite his ups and downs, personally and professionally, he had a keen sense of his rakish appeal to the general public and was willing to use his celebrity not only to support his lifestyle but also to support causes greater than himself.

I first met Curtis in 1988 in Budapest at ceremonies for the dedication of a memorial sculpture to the 600,000 Hungarian Jews murdered in the Holocaust. Imre Varga's weeping-willow-like monument, *Memorial of the Martyrs,* stands to this day in the courtyard of the Dohány Synagogue. The Emanuel Foundation, which Curtis was instrumental in founding and which is named for his father, is a Brooklyn-based charity that sought to preserve and restore sites of Jewish interest in Hungary and had raised money for the memorial. Curtis was in Budapest to garner as much publicity and recognition as possible for the organization and the event and to serve as a draw for local politicians and potential donors.

I was there because my parents were involved in the Emanuel Foundation and because my father was being honored by the Dohány Synagogue for his rescue efforts in Budapest during World War II (a plaque honoring my father's wartime actions is affixed to the base of the Holocaust memorial).

Curtis had traveled to Budapest with two of his children, Kelly and Nick (the latter of whom would later die of a drug overdose). Curtis was charming—the elegance, swagger and air of noblesse oblige that he had employed to pose as a wealthy gentleman in *Some Like It Hot* had by now been absorbed into his public persona. The event was a great success: In the following years, the Dohány Synagogue was completely restored to its pre-war glory with funds from the Hungarian government, and support was being given to other synagogues as well as to maintain Jewish cemeteries all over Hungary.

Several years later, after I moved to Los Angeles, my mother enlisted me to be the driver and general factotum to Andor

Weiss, the Emanuel Foundation's executive director. Weiss was a Brooklyn-based Orthodox rabbi and a Hungarian Holocaust survivor who may have been the most tenacious person I've ever met. Whenever he was in town, I would drive him around, imagining that I was co-starring in a remake of *The Mad Adventures of 'Rabbi' Jacob,* or what would surely one day be the basis for the oddest buddy comedy ever made.

One day, our travels had me turning off Sepulveda Boulevard and into Bel Air Crest. We were directed to a townhouse up the hill. The rabbi, not much more than four feet tall, reached to ring the bell. After a few minutes, the door opened, and there to greet the rabbi was Tony Curtis, wearing short-short white tennis shorts—and nothing else. No shirt, no shoes, his white hair teased high. He embraced the rabbi. Then he turned to me and hugged me, too, before leading us into his home.

We talked for several hours. The rabbi had big plans for Los Angeles: a gala, events, honorees, sponsors. Curtis listened amiably and offered to allow his name to be used on whatever letterhead, committee listing or invitation would help. The rest was up to the rabbi. After that, Curtis took us on a tour of his house. We met his wife, Jill, who bore what seemed an intentional resemblance to Marilyn Monroe but who revealed herself to be her own person—lovely, thoughtful and passionate about horses (in 2009, she and Curtis released a documentary about Shiloh, a horse rescue facility they founded). Everywhere we went, paintings leaned against the walls. Curtis proudly showed us several, talking about the influence of Matisse and Magritte upon his own work, and mentioning upcoming exhibitions of his artwork. Among the works leaning against the walls was one that stood out because of its resemblance to the work of the

Swiss artist Balthus. When asked about it, Curtis confirmed that it was indeed a Balthus—a small work, mixed casually among the Curtis oeuvre.

When we got to the garage, he showed us a new Camaro he'd recently purchased. "When I was a teenager in the Bronx, I loved muscle cars," he said, "and in my head I'm still a teenager who wants his muscle car." You could take the boy out of the Bronx, but it appeared that the Bronx never left the boy. That was what made him a star, allowed him to survive Hollywood, and have a sense of himself that included befriending an Orthodox rabbi and lending his name and his celebrity to raise funds to commemorate his Hungarian Jewish heritage.

And that, for me, was the key to understanding Curtis' lasting appeal: the bald-faced nature of his charm, his vanity, his egotism, all feeding a larger-than-life persona that was self-created and that he deployed with charm and generosity for his benefit and to help others, with his talent sitting there casually in the mix, like a lone Balthus.

October 6, 2010

DEBRIS OF WAR REBORN

The Barzilai Medical Center in Ashkelon in Southern Israel, six miles from Gaza, is a 500-bed facility with an emergency room and a teaching hospital that treats Israelis and Palestinians. Qassam rockets launched from Gaza land so regularly on the building that the top two floors are kept unoccupied as a "safety buffer."

Imagine that you are Lee Wallach, an American and CEO of Community Assets Consulting, a firm specializing in assisting Israeli, international and U.S. environmental technology companies with business in the United States and California. And that you visited Barzilai, some 18 months ago. Or Los Angeles County Sheriff Lee Baca, who, together with his chief of staff, Matt Wollman, also visited Barzilai and, while there, came under rocket attack. Or Niso Maman, an Israeli sculptor of international renown who often works with recycled materials and operates a studio in West Palm Beach, Fla. Or even Daphna Ziman, political activist, philanthropist, founder and chair of Children Uniting Nations, who lives in a beautiful home in Beverly Hills and had heard about Barzilai and the sculptures Maman has created.

Each of these people wanted to do something to help Barzilai.

Here's what happened: Wallach came up with the idea of having an artist create artworks from the missile fragments and debris that had hit the hospital, and he approached Maman, who accepted the challenge. Wallach also approached Baca to discuss how Qassam rocket debris might be allowed into the United States to be fashioned into sculpture and then exhibited. And Ziman offered her home to host a reception for Barzilai, Maman and the sculptures.

All of which is how, on a recent evening, I came to find myself at Ziman's home viewing an exhibition of Maman's sculptures called *The Qassams of Barzilai,* in the company of Maman, Ziman, Wollman and City Councilman Paul Koretz, as well as Dr. Shimon Scharf, Barzilai's CEO and medical director.

Displayed throughout the home were more than a half dozen of Maman's sculptures. They were striking, surprising and challenging. In some instances, the work was humbled by its medium's provenance, at other times it transcended it, becoming a thing of perplexing beauty.

One piece used twisted, rusted strips to form a peace symbol; in another, small shards became a woman's torso. Even more interesting were pieces in which the rocket canister was evident but was surrounded by metal to suggest a futurist-style work of strange energy, a flower of evil, if you will, moving back and forth between horror and beauty. Finally, there were a few sculptures where the metal seemed like mad brushstrokes speaking their own abstract language.

Maman explained that each metal fragment came from shrapnel collected by the Israeli bomb squad, and each had been marked as to when and where it fell, then stored in evidence boxes. "This was the most challenging scrap metal I ever worked with," Maman said. "As an artist, I like challenges. With some pieces I tried to transform them completely," he continued, "but some pieces, it was a struggle to work with the energy of the piece." Maman said his connection to the materials was personal, as he had been in Ashkelon during a rocket attack, and one of the fragments he'd worked with had fallen the day he was there. He said he derived great satisfaction from the work and from the exhibition. "It's a great feeling to do this for the hospital, because they are doing wonderful work," he said.

Wallach said he hopes to send Maman's current exhibit on a national tour and has already garnered support from the American Jewish Committee, StandWithUs and the Iranian American Jewish Group 30 Years After; the latter organization displayed the work during its recent conference at the Century Plaza Hotel. Wallach hopes to invite other artists to "tell the story of Barzilai."

Wallach also has launched a fundraising campaign for the Friends of Barzilai to fund an underground emergency room, protected from attacks; to enhance the hospital's oncology institute; and to renovate the gynecology wing, as well as the neonatal intensive care and pediatric intensive care units. Wallach would like to match the $44 million the Israeli government has pledged for improvements to the hospital.

At the event in her home, Ziman said she had long been frustrated by the situation in Southern Israel and wanted to speak out about the destruction wreaked by the missiles. However, when she first saw the sculptures, she said, "I was blown away." What moved her was that, in "turning death and ugliness into beauty," she saw a powerful metaphor for the best of Israel, that it has been "turning a desert into a garden...building rather than destroying...turning a negative into a positive." She said she was grateful to be able to offer her home for the exhibition.

The event was neither political nor an evening to engender political debate. It was an exhibit of sculptures—interesting, unexpectedly beautiful and poetic. And yet, as Scharf, Barzilai's director, pointed out, no one can look at the sculptures without thinking of the words of Isaiah: "They shall beat their swords into plowshares."

Or, as Maman said, "If shrapnel can be turned into fine art, maybe there's a chance for peace."

October 27, 2010

CHURCHILL'S 'WALK WITH DESTINY'

Who do we have to thank for Hitler's eventual defeat? What was World War II's turning point? Who, by his actions during the war, inspired Chaim Weizmann and David Ben-Gurion, Israel's early leaders? The answer, according to the Simon Wiesenthal Center's stirring new documentary, *Walking With Destiny,* is Winston Churchill.

Churchill, who died in 1965, is hardly a forgotten figure. To the contrary, there is a large and healthy Churchill industry producing new books, one after another, season after season.

To some extent, *Winston Churchill: Walking With Destiny,* which opens November 5 at select Laemmle and Edwards theaters, was born out of historian Martin Gilbert's 2007 work, *Churchill and the Jews* (Gilbert served as a historical consultant to the film). Rabbi Marvin Hier, dean of the Simon Wiesenthal Center and the founder of its Academy Award-winning film division, Moriah Films, along with Richard Trank, the center's media director and Moriah's executive producer, were inspired by the book to make a film that would be, in one sense, larger than a parochial story about Churchill, but in another sense, narrower, focusing on the years 1940 and 1941—as Hier called it, "the most dangerous moment." What Hier wanted to tell was the story of "the man who saved Western civilization."

As Trank explained, the more he got into the research, the more he was struck by how, even into the 1930s, Churchill stood virtually alone in seeing the danger Hitler posed and in speaking out about his revulsion for Hitler's racial policies concerning the Jews. Trank, who also produced and directed *Walking With Destiny*, grew up in Downey, California, the son of one parent who fled the Holocaust just before the war, and the other whose family immigrated earlier to South Africa, where they were Yiddish actors. He earned his bachelor's degree from UC Berkeley and did graduate work at USC. Trank has been the Simon Wiesenthal Center's media director and the executive producer of Moriah Films, the center's Jack and Pearl Resnick Film Division, since 1984. He was the producer of the Academy Award-winning documentary, *The Long Way Home*.

Moriah has often focused on Jewish figures, but *Walking With Destiny* instead profiles a person to whom the Jewish people, as Hier put it, "owe a great debt of gratitude."

The film effectively shows the power of Churchill's uncompromising stance against Hitler—from before the war and during the evacuation of the British Expeditionary Force at Dunkirk, the Battle of Britain and the Blitz—and his efforts to gain the support of President Franklin D. Roosevelt and the reluctant American people.

Still enormously stirring are Churchill's words delivered in his deep, sonorous tones, calling on the British to fight on, casting the conflict in heroic terms, never minimizing the difficulties ahead or how great the stakes were, but assuring the British people that even in the face of death and destruction, they must "carry on." It is hard not to be moved, even today, hearing Churchill's words, and seeing the vintage images of bombed-out, burned and rubble-strewn London.

Here was Churchill, already in his late sixties, a patrician (or, as he might be cast today, "elitist"), ready to lead the people by example, always out in the streets soon after the German bombs fell, talking to people, helping to clear rubble, engaging in the fight, at one with his people—lifting their spirits, hardening their resolve and assuring victory by refusing, alongside them, to be defeated.

Perhaps it's just coincidence that *Walking With Destiny* is being released around the time of the Kristallnacht anniversary. But the message is clear. As Hier put it, without Churchill, nothing that is sacred in Jewish life would have survived.

The relevance to today, although never stated explicitly in the film, is also clear—and this is why I recommend this film whole-heartedly and hope that it will be seen by as many students and schoolchildren as possible. It shows what it means to stand on principle, against all odds in the toughest of times—and that although there are many politicians, only a few are true leaders.

"I would hate to think what the world would be," Hier said, "if there had not been a Winston Churchill."

November 3, 2010

COLUMBO CREATOR SOLVES HIS OWN MYSTERY

"Now, Tom, do I look Jewish?"

William Link, seventy-seven, was asking the question. Link is one of, if not the most successful producer and writer in television history, having put, with his late partner Richard Levinson, sixteen series on the air, including creating *Columbo, Murder, She Wrote, The Cosby Mysteries* and *Mannix.* They also created any number of important TV movies, including *The Execution of Private Slovik,* which launched Martin Sheen's career, *That Certain Summer,* which was the first sympathetic portrayal of gay men on television, and the 1988 *Terrorist on Trial: The United States vs. Salim Ajami,* which was hauntingly prescient.

When I met him, Link was wearing a yellow sweater adorned with dogs, sitting in his art-filled Beverly Hills home with his wife, Marjorie. The answer to his question was not obvious, but the question was being asked with some irony because of Link's situation. His whole life had been spent as a non-Jew, while everyone in his life—his best friend and writing partner, his wife, most of his professional colleagues and associates—all were

Jewish. Yet, a few weeks before we met, Link had discovered that he was, in fact, Jewish.

A man whose past was hidden from him has spent his life writing mysteries. Coincidence? And what of the fact that Link, having turned to writing Columbo short stories, may have solved the two most nagging mysteries in his life—his background, which we might call "The Case of the Blue Suitcase," and another, a question that has dogged him his entire career: How did he and Levinson come up with the name "Columbo" for Peter Falk's character? But more on that later.

There is an episode of *Curb Your Enthusiasm* where, for a brief time, Larry believes he's not Jewish and suddenly becomes un-neurotic, self-confident, a doer, saddled with loving parents and a happy family. This is sort of that story—in reverse.

Link's grandfather walked out on his family when Link's father was thirteen. As a result, Link's father never knew much about his family background. His mother's lineage traced back to the Huguenots, and she spoke German. His father had grown up on the Lower West Side of New York (first tip-off) and was a self-made man, working as a textile broker (second tip-off), and because his father was in a primarily Jewish industry, he spoke some Yiddish (big alarm goes off). Regardless of these indicators, as far as Link is concerned, his father never knew he was Jewish, and Link was raised as a non-Jew. He had a happy childhood and loved his parents.

"They were terrific people, and I miss them to this day," he said.

Link was interested in storytelling even before he could write—he started drawing comic strips as a child. Later, he graduated to writing mystery short stories.

At ten, he was already reading *Weekly Variety* (another clue, perhaps?). On the first day of junior high school, he was told to look out for a tall boy who wrote mysteries and performed magic. Similarly, Levinson was told to look out for a short boy who loved magic and writing mysteries. So began a partnership that lasted forty-three years, until Levinson's death in 1987.

But first, Link played a small part in a Hollywood story. When *Dragnet* premiered as a radio program in 1949, Link recognized the famous opening notes as being the same as the theme from Miklos Rozsa's 1946 *The Killers*. He wrote to the show's composer, Walter Schumann, noting the similarities. Schumann wrote back saying, "Yes, Mr. Link. With Mr. Rozsa's permission, I took the theme from *The Killers*. Keep listening to *Dragnet*."

A while later, when Link read in a front-page story in Variety that Rozsa's music publishers were suing Schumann for plagiarism, he found the letter at the bottom of his closet and gave it to his father, who in turn passed it along to his attorney, who in turn gave it to Rozsa's music publisher. As a reward for Rozsa's victory, Link was invited up to New York to stay at the Plaza hotel, and, as thanks, given tickets to every Broadway musical then playing.

Levinson and Link started writing mystery short stories, and selling them as teenagers to Ellery Queen mystery magazine and Alfred Hitchcock Mystery magazine. They both attended the University of Pennsylvania's Wharton School, but business held no appeal for them. Before the notion of cinema studies was invented, Levinson and Link studied movies and teleplays. Their favorite writer-director was Billy Wilder—they were crazy for anything he did—and their favorite teleplay author was

Paddy Chayefsky. For their college theses, they were allowed to submit "publications," so they submitted three screenplays—all of which they eventually sold. After graduation, the school closed the "publications" loophole.

After serving in the Army and continuing to collaborate on stories via airmail, the two decided to head to Hollywood. Levinson flew ahead, and Link drove cross-country with his good friend Mike Rosenfeld, who would go on to become an agent at William Morris and be one of the founders of Creative Artists Agency (CAA).

Succeeding in television was no angst-filled journey for the duo—their first year, they made $50,000, a fortune in those days, which, according to Link, impressed his mother and made his brother jealous. For the next decade, they freelanced, writing episodes for mystery and drama series of all sorts, from *Johnny Ringo* and *Alfred Hitchcock Presents* to *Honey West, The Fugitive* and *Burke's Law.* And then, in 1968, they adapted a play they had written, *Prescription: Murder,* as a TV movie. It featured a character named Lt. Columbo, played by New York actor Peter Falk. And the rest—well, the rest is not just TV history, but hours and hours of pleasure for families (including mine), generations of writers and shows inspired, and the mentoring and fostering of so many careers, including that of the twenty-one-year-old director of the first on-air episode of the *Columbo* series. What was his name? Oh, yes—Steven Spielberg.

As Link tells it, Lew Wasserman, who ran Universal/MCA, and Sid Scheinberg, who ran Universal TV and would eventually run Universal, showed him and Levinson a short film, *Amblin,* which Spielberg had made, and then asked: "What should we do with this kid?"

"I said, 'Put him under contract,' " Link recalled, "and they did." Link said of Spielberg, "At twenty-one, he was brilliant. He knew every lens. He knew how to move the actors within the frame without having to cut to a close-up. He would only use a close-up when it was important. Spielberg had it all at twenty-one. The nicest guy you ever worked with...and he's that way today."

Levinson died of a heart attack. He had been a three-pack-a-day smoker (four when stressed), and Link, who was with Levinson the day he tried his first cigarette as a teenager, knew that it would one day kill his friend. Levinson knew it, too, "but he was hooked." The loss devastated Link and sent him to a shrink, who helped him continue, and continue to write. But he still feels his partner's presence.

"I think Dick sits on my shoulder, telling me, 'Bill, you can do better with that line.' " TV series, movies and more *Columbo* followed. Link continues to write seven days a week. He no longer writes TV shows, but he still writes mysteries. Stories. And he sells every one.

Recently, Crippen & Landru published Link's *The Columbo Collection,* twelve original short stories featuring Lt. Columbo. Once again, the most persistent detective in the world is hounding the arrogant murderers who think a detective wearing a raincoat in LA is someone they can outsmart. The fact they are—to a person—wrong does not diminish the pleasure of reading how Columbo unravels each crime, often by asking "one more question."

As for how Columbo got his name—for years Link and Levinson were asked that question. For years, they gave an assortment of answers. They couldn't remember. There was a nightclub in Philadelphia called Palumbo's. There was a crime family in New York called Colombo. In the introduction to *The Columbo Collection,* Link offers a theory: Fighter Rocky Marciano's trainer was named Allie Colombo. A.J. Liebling wrote about him, Link watched the fights. Could that be the genesis of the name? Link was not sure.

But when I met him, Link told me confidently that he had finally solved the puzzle. One of Wilder's greatest movies is *Some Like It Hot.* Levinson and Link went to see the film on its opening day in 1959. They studied the screenplay. They watched the film often. But it was only recently that Link was struck by what was staring him in the face all along: The gangster that Curtis and Lemmon are on the run from, played by George Raft, is called, memorably, "Spats."

His full name? "Spats Colombo." Link is now convinced that is the source of the detective's iconic name.

As for that other mystery, the one about Link's Jewish heritage, it turns out that Link's father was troubled by his father's running out on the family and by not knowing anything about him. When Link's father went to serve in Europe in World War II, he hired a genealogist to research his family tree. The report remained in a manila envelope that was placed in a blue suitcase, to which Link's mother added other family documents, such as birth and marriage and confirmation certificates. Upon his mother's death, the blue suitcase passed to Link. He gave it all a cursory look but never examined it thoroughly.

Only recently, Link's niece, Amy, decided to do her own family research and went through the blue suitcase. There, in the old manila envelope, was a family tree, listing Ezekiel, Jacob and Sarah—and, no, the family was not Amish. They were Jewish.

The reaction of most of his friends, thus far, has been, "We always knew." Link says he couldn't be happier. But then again, he's always happy when he's solved a mystery.

February 27, 2011

REMEMBERING ELIZABETH TAYLOR

Elizabeth Taylor, who died Wednesday at age seventy-nine, spent much of her life in the public eye—famous for her violet eyes and her jewelry—and she managed over the years to transition from child star, to legendary beauty, to Oscar-winning actress, to tabloid fodder for her passionate affairs, her tumultuous marriages and divorces, to philanthropist being among the first notable Hollywood personality to speak about AIDS and, as co-founder of AMFAR, one of the earliest AIDS research and support organizations—no small achievement.

Although there have been many books about her, some by Taylor herself, it seemed as if Taylor's own story was too large for one book. She was one of the last Hollywood stars raised in the studio system who knew the old moguls and worked for them. She acted opposite so many great actors, including James Dean, Montgomery Clift and Paul Newman. She was directed by the greats (George Stevens, Jr) and the now great (Mike Nichols). As Dr. Seuss might have said: Oh the things she'd seen!

She was born in London to American parents who moved to Los Angeles in 1939. Her mother, Sara, was an actress with the stage name Sara Sothern and she encouraged her daughter's early career. Taylor was signed by Metro-Goldwyn-Mayer. Her early films included *Lassie Come Home* (1943) with Roddy McDowall and *National Velvet* (1943) with Mickey Rooney, during which she sustained a back injury whose pain would continue to plague her.

By the time she appeared in *Father of the Bride* (1950) she was making her first marriage to Hilton heir Conrad Hilton, Jr., whom she divorced the following year. She then married British actor Michael Wilding in 1952, with whom she had two sons, Michael and Christopher, and whom she divorced in 1957.

Many child actresses find the transition to young woman (and object of desire) difficult.

Elizabeth Taylor turned what appeared on screen as childhood determination into a sultry smoldering presence—in films such as *Cat on a Tin Roof* (1958), *Suddenly Last Summer* (1959), both of which garnered her Oscar nominations, and *Butterfield 8* (1961), playing a call girl, which won her first best actress Oscar.

At the same time, her personal life became the subject of increasingly frenzied press attention. In 1956 she married the producer Mike Todd, whom she proclaimed the love of her life, and they had a daughter Elizabeth Frances. Todd died in a plane crash in 1958. Taylor was distraught. She sought out Todd's Rabbi, Max Nussbaum of Temple Israel of Hollywood, and in 1959 converted to Judaism.

She also began an affair with Eddie Fisher who was then married to Debbie Reynolds. Fisher divorced Reynolds and was married to Taylor—by Rabbi Nussbaum.

Taylor, at the time the biggest movie star in the world, next signed to play *Cleopatra* for a reported $1 million salary (a first for an actress)—a film that turned out to be a fiasco of legendary proportions that almost sank the Fox Studio. Amid the turmoil, Taylor began an affair with her married co-star Richard Burton. However their appearance in *Who's Afraid of Virginia Woolf?* would win Taylor her second Oscar in 1966, as well as a well-received version of *The Taming of the Shrew* (1967).

Their love affair is among Hollywood's most famous. Their dramatic relationship—they married twice, and divorced twice—is the subject of a recent bestseller *Furious Love* by Sam Kashner and Nancy Schoenberger. Their final divorce was in 1975. Taylor would go on to marry (and divorce) both Sen. John Warner and Larry Fortensky, but the romance with Burton would burn brightest.

Taylor continued to act, appearing on Broadway in *The Little Foxes* (1981) and appearing infrequently in movies such as *The Mirror Cracked* (1980). Her last feature appearance was in 1994 as Wilma's mother in the live action movie *The Flintstones.* She did voice work on *The Simpsons* (1992) and *God, the Devil and Bob* (2001).

Taylor checked herself into the Betty Ford Center in 1983 and 1988, again addressing issues that now seem commonplace for celebrities but were not so then.

Taylor also found herself in the role of activist and philanthropist. After her friend, actor Rock Hudson, died of complications related to AIDS, she became one of the first in Hollywood to speak out against the disease—she co-founded AMFAR and raised a reported $50 million to combat the disease.

She was also an early supporter of the Simon Wiesenthal Center, serving on its board of trustees in the 1980s and narrating the center's first documentary, the Oscar-winning *Genocide* (1981).

Taylor was an astute businesswoman, making deals for appearances, and licensing deals regarding perfumes and advertising that kept her in the public eye (and that were quite lucrative). She also garnered frequent tabloid interest for her friendship with Michael Jackson. One of Taylor's last public sightings was at Jackson's memorial.

In Taylor, we have the life of a woman, the story of Hollywood in its golden age and after, a tale of great passion, of enormous heartbreak, an amazing story of great actors, great entertainers, great friendships, a tale of philanthropy, of human weakness, of devastating diseases and a great many untimely deaths, including that of Elizabeth Taylor, Wednesday, at age seventy-nine.

March 24, 2011

FUTURE SHOCK: ALBERT BROOK'S PREDICTS *2030* AMERICA

2*030: The Real Story of What Happens to America* (St. Martin's Press) is Albert Brooks' novel (in all senses of the word) take on our not-so-distant future. Anyone familiar with Brooks' films, such as *Defending Your Life* or *Modern Romance,* will not be surprised that his debut novel is clever and entertaining. But it is also thoughtful, insightful and inventive about issues as diverse as health care, transportation, aging and politics. And funny—let's not forget funny.

2030 is a mixture of the utopian and the dystopian—great advances and great consequences—a future that, even when beyond belief, remains possible.

In *2030,* Brooks takes liberties one imagines he never could have in film to opine on topics large and small (i.e. everyone is tracked everywhere and every birthday party now features an insufferable montage video; the novel ends with a presidential inaugural address).

Brooks also seems to relish the freedom to create a story with no true main character, but, rather, a wide array of figures. They include: Dr. Sam Mueller, who came up with the cure for cancer and reaped the financial benefits of doing so; Matthew Bernstein, the first US president of Jewish descent (his mother is a Roman Catholic, but, as Brooks notes: "If you're running for president, even living on the same street as a Jew makes you one"); Susanna Colbert, a former investment banker Bernstein recruits to be Treasury Secretary and whom he falls for; Brad Miller, an eighty-year-old who ends up buying an apartment on a cruise ship to live out his final years; Max Leonard, a trust-fund-financed revolutionary who wants to harness the anger of young people against the "olds"; and Shen Li, a Chinese health care entrepreneur eager to import his vision of caring neighborhood clinics and surgery performed by robots to the American market.

To Brooks' credit, as each of these characters travels to his or her own date with destiny, the narrative never feels disjointed. We feel we know these characters, and we wonder what's going to happen to them.

Shortly after the novel begins, a 9.1 earthquake occurs on the Pacific Rim (which is scary prescient on Brooks' part), but rather than devastating Asia, it levels Los Angeles. Miller is taken to a tent village in Pasadena to wait for the insurance money that is promised him, but never seems to appear. In the meantime, the country can't afford the trillions of dollars it will take to rebuild Los Angeles. Bernstein sends Colbert to beg the Chinese for a loan. They refuse, but instead propose an equity stake—they will rebuild the city in return for fifty percent of the city's revenues and the pledge that Chinese workers who participate in the rebuilding can become U.S. citizens within two years. In no time, Brooks tells us, Los Angeles smells "better."

Brooks empathizes with his characters and does not judge their foibles too harshly, as if to say, "Nobody's perfect." The novel has no truly evil characters, and in *2030,* as Jean Renoir once famously remarked, "Everyone has their reasons." Brooks' characters remain entertaining even in their darkest moments—as when Leonard has lunch with Walter Master, a Jack Kevorkian-type euthanasia advocate, who tells him, "Go change the world. I'll pay for the sandwich."

On the other hand, Brooks is clear that there is always a price to pay for our actions. When the Nobel Prize-winning billionaire Mueller disses Leonard, the latter conceives a plot that will have tragic implications for others, including Miller; Bernstein's re-election will hinge on whether Colbert pays back a favor to a large contributor, as well as on Bernstein's wife's reaction to his feelings for Colbert. In Brooks' world of tomorrow, much like our present, human self-interest still clouds our judgment and chance meetings can still lead to outcomes we can never foresee.

That Brooks enjoyed writing this book is evident on every page, and that, too, is infectious. Although, as a filmmaker, his comedies have always taken a close look at relationships and at society, at times played out to surreal extremes, in this first novel, Brooks has found a medium particularly well suited to his polymath interests and prolific inventiveness. Although living in 2030 may be more difficult than now in many respects, reading about it is very enjoyable. Or as Brooks recently tweeted: "Medical Breakthrough: *2030* increases lifespan! (of author, but still)."

May 10, 2011

DEMJANJUK SENTENCED

John Demjanjuk, circa 1943, has been convicted of being an accessory to the murder of 29,700 Jews at the Sobibor death camp in Poland.

The conviction today of John Demjanjuk, ninety-one, by a German court is significant in many respects, not the least of which is that this may be one of the last Nazi war crimes trials.

Demjanjuk was freed pending appeal, having been found guilty of being an accessory to the murder of more than 28,000 Jewish men, women and children at the Sobibor extermination camp, having been trained at the Trawniki camp in Nazi-occupied Poland. He was convicted primarily on the basis of documentary evidence, records of his service at several camps, including his identification card from the Trawniki camp. At the trial, relatives of those murdered at Sobibor during the time Demjanjuk served there confirmed their family members' place on the train transports that took them to their deaths. Demjanjuk was sentenced to five years in jail and was released pending appeal.

By trying Demjanjuk, who was born in Soviet-era Ukraine and served the Germans in Nazi-occupied Poland, Germany makes the point that its moral and legal responsibility for trying crimes of the Nazi era does not end at Germany's present borders, and that the Germans recruited willing non-German participants to aid in the murder of the Jews, who bear responsibility for their actions.

Judge Ralph Alt, the presiding judge, was quoted as saying "Every Trawniki man knew that he was part of a well and smoothly operating apparatus that had no other goal than systematically murdering Jews. They all knew about the barbaric treatment of Jews. And the accused was part of that extermination machinery."

This is the latest, but possibly not the last, chapter in the Demjanjuk legal saga, which reaches back to the mid-1970s, when Demjanjuk, then an immigrant Cleveland auto-worker, was first accused of being a former Nazi guard. Trials ensued in the United States, stripping him of his citizenship, ordering him deported, and then extradited to Israel, where he was prosecuted in the late 1980s in a public trial that sought to prove that in addition to serving at Trawniki and Sobibor, he was also the sadistic gas chamber operator at Treblinka, called "Ivan The Terrible." When, on appeal, testimonies from the former Soviet Union pointed to another person being the gas chamber operator at Treblinka, Israel's Supreme Court ordered the release of Demjanjuk, based on reasonable doubt, and although it was affirmed that he was at Trawniki and Sobibor, Israeli courts declined to hold or retry him on those charges—a decision that was seen as speaking to Israel's fairness. Back in the United States, the government was forced to begin their case anew, once again denaturalizing Demjanjuk and ordering him deported to Germany. And that is where he has now been tried and convicted.

The persistence of the governments of the United States (throughout both Republican and Democratic administrations), Israel and Germany in pursuing this case over the years is to be commended. Through it all, Demjanjuk has denied his involvement, and at each turn the evidence and the courts have put truth to his lie. When they found a criminal before them, they prosecuted him.

Demjanjuk sentence is five years in prison, taking into account his age, his prison time in Israel and the fact that having been denaturalized of his United States citizenship, he was separated from his family. Given his advanced age and the fact that the appeals on his behalf could take up to a year, there is some question as to whether Demjanjuk will ever enter prison. The German prosecutor is considering appealing the decision to release Demjanjuk.

Has justice been served with this mere five year sentence (even for someone aged ninety-one) plus the fact that Demjanjuk is currently free on appeal in Germany Justice? Is this a fitting, or even satisfying, end to the decades-long prosecution of a participant in the murder of thousands of Jewish men women and children?

I am still struggling with this odd calculus of German crime and punishment, but only time will tell how this story ends—the last page is still not written. However, I can still recall sitting in the courtroom in Jerusalem more than two decades ago, watching Demjanjuk for many days on end. The crimes described seemed to me to have taken place on another planet. Yet here before us was the tangible evidence, the documents, the records, the witnesses from that place. Here was another generation standing in court to say that a nation of laws trumps a nightmare of evil. The verdict today affirms that.

We live in a time when opinions are often taken as facts and when the torrent of commentary online in real time can overwhelm. Demjanjuk's attorneys and supporters will continue to proclaim his innocence or denounce the evidence as forgeries. But as of today, Demjanjuk once again bears the mark of Cain, as his guilt has been pronounced in a legal process carried out by German authorities in a courtroom in Munich—the very city where Hitler founded the Nazi party.

If the Nazis or their henchmen thought the world would forget their crimes, or not care, they have been proven wrong once again.

May 12, 2011

HAPPY BIRTHDAY, BOB!

That Hibbing, Minn., native who was born Robert Allen Zimmerman but has been known as Bob Dylan since he first started performing in New York's Greenwich Village some fifty years ago—and who has lived in Los Angeles probably longer than anywhere else—turns seventy on May 24.

Like most Dylan-related matters, this defies logic and the laws of time and space. If, to quote the birthday boy, "Love is just a four-letter word," then what is age other than three letters strung together?

However, three score and ten years is not just any birthday, as the psalms note—it is a milestone, and a celebration is very much in order. But how should we celebrate?

We could send the Bobster a card or drop him a note. But what is there to say to the man who has said and sung it all; performed on stages large and small, in every country all over the world; whose music plays in every nook and cranny where sound can be heard; whose songs and lyrics are the soundtrack of events both personal and historic, of adolescence and maturity, of love and heartbreak, of a wisdom that seems within grasp and eludes us; who remains a touchstone and cipher all at the same time; and has for more than fifty years of performing in public?

We could celebrate by singing one of his songs. But which one? At seventy, Dylan has written more songs than Woody Guthrie, Lead Belly or all his idols combined and had a career that has lasted longer than he or anyone could have imagined. Whenever he has reached what seemed an impasse—personally, musically or even spiritually—he has found a way to continue to perform, record and write songs.

Furthermore, is there another living artist whose songs are covered by as many performers? Perhaps his songs remain evergreen and current for just those reasons that his critics fault him—because Dylan's songs sometimes defy literal meaning. Or because they often appear on his albums as a work in progress, they always remain open to an artist's fresh interpretation.

We could stage a reading. For decades, Dylan gave cryptic interviews offering no evidence that he could string a coherent paragraph together. But more recently he has opened himself up to documentaries and to a series of conversations where he has, as best he could, tried to leave a fuller record and create context for his work. More to the point, he wrote a memoir, *Chronicles, Volume 1,* which is as generous as it is well crafted, one of the best accounts of an artist finding his voice. Beyond that, Dylan has engendered a shelf worth of books.

We could donate to a cause. Despite rejecting early calls to be a leader, Dylan has helped causes large (FarmAid) and small (the Chabad Telethon) as well as artists and individuals. When Patti Smith needed to return to touring, Dylan offered her an opening spot. Doesn't sound like much, but it made all the difference to her.

We could go see him perform. Although Dylan has been on what has been called "the never-ending tour" for more than two decades, a quick glance at the calendar on his Web site shows no performance dates for May—and none on his birthday. Hmmm. So what's a fan to do?

Let's begin by saying: Thank you. Thank you for the songs and for the music, for the time performing. Because, as you noted in your first song to Woody, "There's not many men who've done the things that you've done." As you turn seventy, we're not going to wish that you stay "Forever Young," but we wish that in the words of your song, "may your heart always be joyful" and "may your song always be sung." I know I'll be listening to your songs on the radio and on my iPod now and for many years to come. So what else is there to say, other than—all together now—"Happy Birthday, Bob!"

If you want to celebrate Bob Dylan's birthday, there are various film, music and print tributes you can enjoy, including visiting rollingstone.com's "Happy 70th Birthday, Bob!" page complete with a quiz, interviews, photo galleries, etc.

My favorite Dylan albums: *Blood on the Tracks, Highway 61 Revisited, Slow Train Coming* and *Bringing It All Back Home.* My favorite Dylan album that no one else listens to: *Street Legal* (I had a cassette and played it incessantly on a cross-country trip long ago). Favorite song from a Dylan album no one listens to: "Shot of Love."

My favorite Dylan songs of relatively recent vintage: "Thunder on the Mountain," "Mississippi," "Workingman's Blues No. 2," "Shooting Star," "Things Have Changed" "Everything Is Broken" and "Not Dark Yet."

My favorite cover versions of Dylan songs: Eric Clapton, "Don't Think Twice, It's All Right"; Sheryl Crow, "Mississippi"; Jimi Hendrix, "All Along the Watchtower" and "Like a Rolling

Stone"; Shawn Colvin, "Buckets of Rain"; Madeleine Peyroux, "You Going to Make Me Lonesome When You Go"; The O'Jays, "Emotionally Yours"; Doug Sahm and Band, "Wallflower"; and Johnny Winter, "Highway 61 Revisited."

Most eccentric covers I ever heard Dylan perform in concert: Dion's "Abraham, Martin and John" and Jimmy Buffett's "A Pirate Looks at Forty" (both in the same night).

May 24, 2011

BEAUTY IS SKIN DEEP

On the afternoon I attended the Annenberg Space for Photography's latest exhibition, *Beauty Culture*, I was standing in the dark watching a series of fashion images projected in the digital gallery, when I was distracted by a woman who entered the room. I did a double take, as I recognized her as one of the iconic women featured in the exhibition, a former fashion model.

My eyes darted between looking at her watching herself and looking at the images of her on the screen. In the pictures, she was an otherworldly creature, a two-dimensional slate on which to project beauty, an object lesson in perfection, created in the service of commerce. In person, she stood aloof from her image, disengaged, cool but somehow timid—as, if in the dark, the photo was real and she was the shadow.

Lauren Greenfield, a Los Angeles-born-and-based photographer and documentarian, had created a specially commissioned film for the exhibit, and it was about to start. The model withdrew, and I stayed.

Greenfield's thirty-minute film explores the cult of beauty from several viewpoints—of the photographers, such as Albert Watson, Melvin Sokolsky and Tyen; of models, among them

Crystal Renn, Emme and Carmen Dell'Orefice; of modeling agents, such as Eileen Ford and Bethann Hardison; of young women (beauty pageant contestants, teenagers, body builders); of plastic surgeons; and of women who have had plastic surgery or cosmetic enhancements, including Cindy Margolis (the self-anointed most downloaded woman on the Internet). It also interviews New York Times reporter Alex Kuczynski, author of *Beauty Junkies,* as well as a French intellectual who had cheek implants inserted at eyebrow level, and actress Jamie Lee Curtis, who derides unreal cosmetic enhancements and who asks: "What is with the lip thing?"

Beauty Culture also displays 175 print images from 100 photographers, both commercial and fine artists. Among them are Vogue celebrity photographer Bert Stern, the Surrealist Man Ray, ad-campaign and portrait artist Herb Ritts, the French fashion photographer Guy Bourdin, Rolling Stone and Interview celebrity portraitist Matthew Rolston, the German eroticist Ellen von Unwerth, the feminist artist Leonard Nimoy (yes, that Leonard Nimoy) and the French commercial graphic/photographic illustrator Jean-Paul Goude. The show also explores a variety of topics, including Hollywood glamour, the continuing influence of Marilyn Monroe's short career, the artifice integral to the billion-dollar cosmetics industry, the modeling industry, and a view of some iconic women who have come to embody a moment or era, including Jean Shrimpton, Twiggy, Cheryl Tiegs, Christy Turlington, Kate Moss and Gisele Bundchen.

The exhibition also asks: What size is beautiful? What color is beautiful? And it investigates the phenomenon of the pin-up girl, from Betty Grable to Farrah Fawcett, as well as women who have used images of androgyny to advantage. There's also a section called “Reaction and Revolution,” which explores how retouching creates ideals of beauty unattainable even by the subjects. And, on the other side, it shows ways in which photographers, models and individuals have revolted against such narrow definitions of beauty.

“As much as beauty can astonish and inspire,” Wallis Annenberg, of the Annenberg Foundation, is quoted as saying in a press release for the exhibition, “it can also corrupt and subvert, rendering all else—even itself—broken and obsolete. The great contemporary photographers…turn art’s mirror on ourselves as well. I can’t think of a more important conversation for the Annenberg Space to have.”

But is this exhibition really a conversation? The images are presented like a runway procession of our cultural fixations, a progression of beauties, actresses and models whom we’ve come to know by name and whose celebrity has increased in parallel with the success of the products and industries at whose service they made their fortunes. The images are beautiful, even when the subject is not (such as one picture of a needle being applied for a collagen injection).

The exhibition asks worthy questions about the sexualization of children; about a definition of beauty that more often than not depicts a white, skinny, youthful girl, while in the real world, standards of beauty have moved away from the blond, blue-eyed waiflike tomboy to more athletic, more curvy, more ethnic beauties. It asks about how our own self-image is impacted by a world where even the most beautiful women are digitally doctored—to lengthen their legs, or remove the wrinkles or blemishes from their faces.

These are certainly valid questions, but not surprises.

And, sometimes just asking the questions is not enough. *Beauty Culture* left me feeling empty—it simply skims the surface of the issues by acknowledging them, while the very beauty of the images acts as a counterargument, one that says: That's just the way it is. No matter the importance of Oprah or popularity of J.Lo or the successes of the Kardashians, modeling agents will continue to stand outside of high schools in Brazil or the Baltic countries looking for a fourteen-year-old beauty to sign to a modeling contract.

Cosmetic and jeans companies will not sign the winners of the Westinghouse science competition, or even the national spelling bee, to be their spokespersons. The cult of beauty is about the ideals and values attributed to a world of surfaces.

After staring at the model staring at herself in that dark room, I was hoping for an epiphany, an insight into the deeper nature of the transaction we enact in conferring the status of beauty upon an image or a person. I had none, and the exhibit provided nothing more.

On the subject of imbuing meaning, Sigmund Freud supposedly said, "Sometimes a cigar is just a cigar." And sometimes a model looking at a photo of herself is just a person looking at a picture.

June 21, 2011

EVERY PICTURE HAS A STORY

For thirty years, Michael Schwartz has owned and operated Galerie Michael, an art gallery on Rodeo Drive in Beverly Hills, building, in his own words, "museum-quality collections, one work at a time." Works by Picasso, Dali, Goya and Miró adorn the walls for the current exhibition on Spanish masters.

With a staff of twenty-four, many of whom hold fine-arts degrees and are called curators, Schwartz would be happy to sell you a work of art. But he would prefer to tell you a story first because what Schwartz really wants to do is enchant you.

I've known a few art dealers in my time, and much the way poker players have a tell, dealers have a "sell." Some dealers sell status and exclusivity—as if you are joining a club; others make a more mercenary pitch, appealing to one's sense of value, investment savvy and greed; for others, the sell is more aesthetic, with a focus on the artist's technique, or on occasion how the painting matches the client's home. Schwartz's sell is different: He wants to educate you.

Which is funny because until he became an art dealer, Schwartz didn't know all that much about art. He grew up in Chicago. His mother, who had been trained as a concert pianist but took on more commercial gigs once she had children, was always taking her children to museums and stressing the importance and beauty of art.

By his thirties, Schwartz was in charge of circulation for Look magazine in several Midwestern states, when his boss started taking him to Europe. At the same time, some friends approached him with the idea of opening a gallery in Chicago that would appeal to recent college graduates and other young people starting out in life who wanted to buy good art but could only afford prints. They asked Schwartz to buy them a Picasso the next time he was in Paris.

Schwartz wandered into a gallery and explained that he was in search of a Picasso for a gallery in Chicago. The owner asked what he knew about prints and paintings. "Not much," Schwartz said. The gallery owner took an interest in Schwartz and started to teach him that every painting has a story that makes it come alive. The gallery owner told Schwartz that this time he would select the best work for him to buy, but that he needed to study the artists and their work; the next time, Schwartz would have to choose. Thus began his art education.

Back in Chicago, Schwartz's wife was becoming impatient with his investment. Her ultimatum: Have them pay you back or take the painting. It was right around then that Schwartz had an epiphany: He loved art and would open his own gallery. Although he had four young children, his wife gave him a year to establish himself—which he did. However, during the winter of 1978, Chicago was beset by a blizzard so severe that Schwartz was barely able to see the road as he drove home. He pulled over at a diner and called his wife: "I've had it. I'm leaving." His wife told him he was having a midlife crisis and that they should try to work out their problems. Schwartz explained that he didn't want to leave her—he wanted to leave Chicago and move the family to California.

After a few months of due diligence, Schwartz found a gallery in South Coast Plaza that was foundering and made an offer to acquire its inventory and take it over. He bought a home for his family here and enrolled his kids in school for the coming year. A few days before closing, the gallery owner informed Schwartz that he had sold to a higher bidder. "But we had a deal!" Schwartz protested. "I moved my family to California!" The gallery owner said he was sorry but their deal was not finalized. Schwartz sued.

The following week, Schwartz found himself wandering in Beverly Hills, on Rodeo Drive. There he found a beautiful building next to the Hermès store that was a showroom for the Beverly Park development, then in its early stage. Schwartz loved the space. He called his wife and told her that he felt their future was in Beverly Hills, on Rodeo Drive. Even more, he felt as if that space was meant for them. "The energy there was fantastic," he said. Schwartz, who describes himself as a BuJew (Jewish Buddhist), threw the I Ching as well—it, too, confirmed that his future was in Beverly Hills.

Nine months later, having spent a tidy sum on litigation to no result, Schwartz got a call from a real estate broker. There was a space available on Rodeo Drive, but the owner insisted on meeting directly with all prospective tenants. Schwartz soon found himself in the space he had coveted—the real estate development had sold out in record time. The owner had many demands; Schwartz had a few of his own. What Schwartz suggested was that they each write down on separate legal pads what they needed in order to make the sale—then they switched pads. In ten minutes, they had a deal. "It was bashert," Schwartz now says.

For the next twenty-eight years, Schwartz operated his gallery there to great success. He continued to travel to Europe, establishing long-standing relationships with important dealers, including members of the Pissaro, Renoir and Cezanne families. In keeping with the European gallery tradition, Schwartz sought to distinguish himself by organizing exhibitions and publishing catalogs, making his gallery a place to learn about and buy affordable art. Although Schwartz estimates that sixty percent of his work sells for between $10,000 and $50,000, he still offers works by Picasso for as little as $3,000 (even though he knows that is, in itself, a lot of money).

Two years ago, when Schwartz could not come to terms with his landlord (Schwartz wanted a ten-year lease; his landlord wanted to give him four), he moved to the former José Eber hair salon space on Via Rodeo—a larger space for less money with a long lease. He feels that the space brings its own excitement.

On Rodeo Drive, over the decades, he has watched the ebb and flow of commerce, from the Drexel Burnham traders of the 1980s to the current wave of Internet entrepreneurs. He has seen waves of buyers come and go, from the Middle East, Japan, Russia and China. Schwartz estimates that sixty percent of his business is based on repeat customers.

"Being here [on Rodeo] is a multinational experience," Schwartz said.

Schwartz has come to believe that although Los Angeles in general, and Beverly Hills in particular, are not art destinations like New York, many of its visitors are art collectors. And, he said, if they visit Rodeo Drive, as they inevitably do, they are often surprised to find a gallery like his there, with the quality works he exhibits.

Over the years, Schwartz's areas of interest have been nineteenth century plein air painting (landscapes); old master drawings, with a particular interest in Rembrandt; and works by such twentieth century masters as Picasso, Miró and Dali. Schwartz curated the Kaplan collection of Rembrandt artworks exhibited in England and Germany. He also has an expertise in the graphic works of Toulouse-Lautrec and was instrumental in bringing the Wagner collection of French poster art to LACMA's permanent collection.

Schwartz's fundamental belief is that knowledge surrounds a work, deepening the viewer's connection to it. To demonstrate this, he showed me a small Renoir work, a scrap the painter had used to sketch a face—Schwartz told me about the girl it was based on, how Renoir used these scraps and how rare they are. As he did, I looked at the work anew, finding delight in details I might otherwise have missed. Yet, to be completely honest, I would say that Schwartz's charm in telling those stories is as great a factor as the knowledge he imparts.

Schwartz also recounted how once, when he went to visit Dali at his home in Spain, he was ushered into a garden where the aged Surrealist was sitting on a throne, dressed like a pope, wearing a large ring that Dali's assistant told Schwartz he should kiss. Schwartz refused, but instead opened a briefcase full of cash and asked if that might serve as his acknowledgement of Dali's genius. Dali consented, and Schwartz proposed that Dali do an edition of works based on the many inventions that Dali had conceived, including a reclining massage chair that replicated the feeling of being a baby in the womb. Dali told Schwartz that the idea was not Schwartz's but Dali's, because he had inspired him to have this idea. The edition was very successful. Schwartz still has a set and promised to show them to me. I thanked him but said no. I had to go.

I was afraid this might turn out to be a very expensive column.

August 9, 2011

HOW LA GREW ITS OWN ART

For those of us who are not native to Los Angeles yet live here (some for more of our lives than anywhere else), there is a compulsion to define Los Angeles, to get control in some manner of this ever-changing city that is distinguished as much by its sprawl as its particulars, by its air and light as its buildings and institutions, by its self-made individualists as its patchwork of ethnic communities.

It is in this spirit of examining dichotomies that, beginning in October and for the six months that follow, Los Angeles and its surrounding communities will be home to *Pacific Standard Time: Art in LA 1945-1980,* an enormously ambitious attempt to make sense of the ephemeral and tangible through exhibitions at more than 60 museums, galleries and various other sites from Santa Barbara to San Diego. The project will also reach Pasadena and Pomona, as well as Palm Springs, with a 10-day arts festival slated for its mid-point in January.

This enormous undertaking, initiated and overseen by the Getty Research Institute (GRI), makes the case for the many ways in which Los Angeles has been a partner, catalyst and home to a unique, prolific and influential artistic vision. *Pacific Standard Time* is nothing more or less than a declaration of the importance of Los Angeles to the narrative of post-World War II American art. Its ambition is not only to reset how the art world views Los Angeles, but how we, who live here, view our own city—beyond Hollywood, Rodeo Drive, the freeways and the beaches.

The project's genesis dates back about a decade, according to Andrew Perchuk, GRI deputy director. Perchuk and Rani Singh, a GRI senior research associate, as well as the GRI's then-director Tom Crow, who left in 2007, all arrived at the Getty around 2000. Crow was a California native, and all three were interested in learning more about the art of Southern California. In what might be described as a "Big Yellow Taxi" moment, they realized "people were dying, and the history was fast disappearing," Perchuk said.

"The Getty Research Institute [launched] a big oral-history research project to capture the first-person perspectives of the artists, curators, collectors, dealers and other people in the art scene. At the same time, Nancy Kienholz [widow and collaborator of Ed Kienholz] and [the now-deceased painter and museum director] Henry Hopkins approached the Getty Foundation to encourage them to preserve the paper record, the archival record." The Getty subsequently commissioned a survey of archives related to Southern California. The institutions holding those archives were then able to make proposals and receive grants from the Getty to catalogue and make accessible their collections to scholars. The Getty also started collecting heavily in the archival area of the postwar years.

"We realized that we had uncovered so much interesting and new information…that we came up with the idea of a series of exhibitions," Singh said. They brought that idea to a number of institutions, including the Los Angeles County Museum of Art (LACMA), the Museum of Contemporary Art (MOCA) and the Hammer Museum.

It quickly became clear, Singh said, that "Everyone had very interesting ideas and a very deep wealth of information and exhibition material…It very quickly snowballed into something [where] no one [exhibit] was overlapping in any way or stepping on anyone else's toes. Everybody's idea was unique and specific, and they had eked out their own corner of the story that is Los Angeles."

The Getty gave grants in two phases, one for research and planning and then for the actual exhibitions and publications. The result is a citywide collaboration, the likes of which Los Angeles has not seen since the 1984 Olympics. Although it will be nearly impossible to attend every exhibit or event related to *Pacific Standard Time* it will be hard not to be taken with the extent of creativity and artistry born in the region.

Pacific Standard Time will explore the hard-edged pop art (think Ed Ruscha) and assemblage works (Ed Kienholz) that made a name for Los Angeles in the 1960s, as well as the minimalist (such as Robert Irwin) and conceptual (Chris Burden) artists who followed them; the émigré architects (including Rudolf Schindler) who put their stamp on postwar LA; and the Chicano, feminist and African American artists who struggled to have their work acknowledged.

The Museum of Natural History, LACMA's first home (then called The Los Angeles County Museum of History, Science, and Art) will show California artists from 1945 to 1963, while the Getty Museum's own exhibit, *Crosscurrents in LA Painting and Sculpture, 1950–1970* will feature an overview that, Perchuk said, "finds an interesting way to present some old favorites, some great paintings by David Hockney and Ed Ruscha, some rediscoveries like the amazing resin paintings of Ron Davis, and some [work] not particularly well recognized even in its own era, like some of the assemblage [by] artists like Ron Miyashiro." The GRI will focus on how artists such as Wallace Berman, George Herms, Chris Burden, Judy Chicago and John Baldessari disseminated their messages to the public. MOCA will present *Under the Big Black Sun: California Art 1974-1981*, the most comprehensive survey of that period in Los Angeles art to date, bracketed by the resignation of Richard Nixon and the election of Ronald Reagan.

The Hammer will offer the work of African American artists in the postwar era, while The Autry National Center of the American West will exhibit the work of Mexican American artists such as Hernando Villa, Alberto Vades and Roberto Chavez; the Chinese American Museum will present the work of Chinese American architects in Los Angeles during the period; the Craft and Folk Art Museum will feature the work of living-legend enamellist June Schwarcz. And the Grammy Museum will focus on the music scene here from 1945 to 1970. The list goes on and on, literally, and can be examined in great detail at pacificstandardtime.org/participants.

There will be special regional weekends, shuttle buses, special T-shirted volunteers.

This thing is huge.

Yet as vast as *Pacific Standard Time* will be, it is also going to be personal. It is about artists and the prisms through which they view the world; it is about inspiration, cross-pollination and the personalities that have made Los Angeles a place where artists chose to work. What I learned in reading just the press materials for *Pacific Standard Time* and through my conversations with Getty officials, is that in order for artists to make Los Angeles their own, they needed not just a sense of community, but also support—collectors who would become champions of their work, as well as art dealers and, ultimately, museums to show their work. By that measure, one of the least heralded but most important catalysts to the Los Angeles art scene was Stanley Grinstein, one of the founders of Gemini G.E.L. (Graphic Editions Limited); he and his wife, Elise, have often been hailed as "the godparents of the LA art scene."

Recently I met Grinstein in his art-filled Brentwood home, where he recounted for me his own involvement in the scene here.

Grinstein, born in 1927, grew up in Seattle. "We always went to the Seattle Art Museum, but we didn't take it too seriously," he recalled. He had some relatives who were, in his words, "Bohemian"—and he got a sense that that was where the parties were. His whole family moved to Los Angeles when he was 16, and he went to USC.

"Even at USC," he said, "we knew about the art scene." He married Elise, who painted and held art classes.

Grinstein went into the forklift business and became active in the Young Men's Club at Cedars-Sinai. As he tells it, one day, someone came around and told them that many of the Jewish organizations in the city were looking for new leadership and offered to expose them to their choice of organization. Grinstein chose the Westside Jewish Community Center, in part because at the time he lived nearby, in Carthay Circle.

The JCC, Grinstein said, "turned out to be very interesting." Every year they held a fundraiser, an art fair of sorts drawn from various artists and galleries. "We had a group that was very into art," he said. For many, it was an introduction to contemporary art. Among the artists who participated were the conceptualists Allen Ruppersberg, Bruce Nauman and Michael Asher.

At the same time, curators were reaching out as well to develop new collectors. Grinstein and his wife took classes in contemporary art from Walter Hopps (co-founder of the groundbreaking Ferus Gallery and, later, director of the Pasadena Art Museum) and from Hopps' wife, Shirley.

Collectors Fred and Marcia Weisman recommended the Grinsteins join the contemporary art council of LACMA, when the museum was still housed in Exposition Park. Jim Elliott, who later went on to UC Berkeley, exposed them to such experimental, multimedia artists as John Cage.

Elise was on the new talent committee, and she and Eugenia Butler were going out to meet young artists in their studios.

The Grinsteins became more involved in collecting and purchased a major painting by Josef Albers.

Somewhere around 1965 they became friendly with the sculptor Larry Bell. For the gala opening of the new mid-Wilshire LACMA, the Grinsteins invited Bell as their guest. Doing so gave them the seal of approval among artists.

The Grinsteins tried having dinner parties with artists, but they were a failure; the artists were concerned the Grinsteins would just be using them to show off to their friends. So, instead, they decided to have parties for the artists to invite their friends. There was no set pattern, but they happened pretty much once a month, and there was always some excuse for them—an artist was having a show in town, or they would make up a reason. One of the more legendary parties was one in honor of a sumo competition in town, where the sumo wrestlers showed up.

Over the years, a fair amount of artists were known to overindulge a bit, but never to excess (although one did have to be tied up when he became enraged over his wife leaving the party with someone else). The only bad thing that happened was that a small work by Wallace Berman once disappeared during a get-together (and it has never resurfaced). The Grinsteins hesitated over telling Berman, with whom they'd become close. When they finally did, all he said was, "Boy, someone must have really wanted it!"

Sid Felsen was an accountant whom Grinstein had befriended in college—they were both members of the ZBT fraternity at USC, when Felsen was there as a returning veteran. Felsen took art classes from Grinstein's wife and was part of their art group. He also did a lot of tax returns for artists. Felsen and Grinstein were approached about opening an art auction house, but they decided against it. Still, they wanted to be closer to the artists. "One day, we said to each other: 'Maybe prints? Maybe we could do prints out here,'" Grinstein recalled.

They had brought a lot of prints to the Westside Jewish Community Center. Grinstein had come to know Ken Tyler, who was a master printer at Tamarind Lithography Workshop. He invited him to a Christmas party and asked if he wanted to launch a print center that he would back, along with Felsen. Tyler agreed; now all they needed was the artists.

They began by approaching older artists, such as Edward Hopper, who offered a plate to restrike an existing work, which they refused (Grinstein says he regrets that now—he surmises he would have gotten Hopper to do something to the plate), as well as Mark Rothko and Barnett Newman, who said yes, in principle, but they were busy and told them to wait (Rothko never did any prints for them). At that point, Grinstein turned to Tyler and suggested they try Albers, whom Tyler had worked with and whose work Grinstein collected. Albers said yes. But it would take a year before the print was done.

The delay gave them time to look elsewhere. The Surrealist Man Ray (born Emmanuel Radnitzky) was staying with the Grinsteins, and although by this time he had become bitter, they got him to do some prints; they also got some from social-activist artist Ben Shahn. For a while they tried to entice some of the Mexican and Chicano artists, but without success.

When the Albers print finally came out, it sold well—at $100 a print. Still, they needed a $10,000 bank loan to keep things going. Felsen didn't quit his accounting job for many years, and Grinstein never gave up the forklift company.

A turning point occurred when Robert Rauschenberg decided to visit Los Angeles in the spring of 1967. The artist had been taking a break from painting after showing at the Venice Biennale and had started a roller-skating dance troupe (Rauschenberg actually performed on roller skates with the Judson Dance Theater). Rauschenberg wanted to make wings out of steel, and Grinstein, being in the forklift business, was able to get the artist what he needed. Grinstein then asked if Rauschenberg would come to Los Angeles and make some prints here. He agreed.

"That was our breakthrough," Grinstein recalled, "Once he came out, we had a direction, and all the other Castelli artists came out. That put Gemini G.E.L. on the map." When Jasper Johns agreed to do a series at Gemini, Gemini became financially viable.

As Grinstein explained, "When you went to New York, you could go to Max's Kansas City the first night and see half the art world there." In Los Angeles, there was no equivalent outside of a group of artists who showed at the Ferus Gallery hanging out at Barney's Beanery.

East Coast artists began to come to Los Angeles to work at Gemini, and they met local artists either at the print studio or at one of the Grinstein's parties, and thus the scene grew. Early on, Gemini made works with Sam Francis, Ruscha, Robert Graham, Larry Bell and Wallace Berman, among others. Grinstein would often turn to artists such as Chuck Arnoldi and Laddie John Dill (who worked as an apprentice printer at Gemini) to start the word of mouth about a party.

Grinstein feels that from the beginning Los Angeles had a lot to offer the artists. "There's the light—some people say that art is how you deal with light." Grinstein also believes that the studio space available to artists impacted the very conception of their art here. Finally, he feels there was some benefit for artists who chose not to be in New York—they could create outside of the spotlight. Grinstein became close to many of them, including Wallace Berman, whom he found to be a spiritual soul, a pure hippie (Berman died young, the victim of a car crash). At the entrance to Grinstein's home stands *Topanga Seed*, by Berman.

Grinstein also gave financial support to artists, opening up house accounts at art supply stores in the area to pay for their supplies. When Judy Chicago started to do environmental constructions, Grinstein gave her one of his forklifts to make the work. He also let several artists work out of his forklift company's site, including Judy Chicago and Mark Di Suervo.

Equally important, Grinstein and Felsen stood by artists at all phases of their careers, and both Gemini G.E.L. editions and the Grinsteins' own art collection reflect that. Grinstein essentially let the artists be part of his family. Man Ray, Allen Ginsberg and Philip Glass would only come to Los Angeles if they could stay at the Grinsteins' house. As Glass said, in a documentary being made about the Grinsteins, a clip of which can be found on YouTube: "They were not bystanders…Their activities were aligned with development, preservation of art and the encouragement of artists to come and work here. They weren't just hosts to the community; they were actively involved in it."

Looking back, Grinstein now says: "I was proud of all the artists—we felt so lucky each time they made a work for us."

For *Pacific Standard Time* Gemini G.E.L. is offering a chronological exhibit of their output. Like the full collection of shows that will proliferate around the region for *Pacific Standard Time*, they tell the story of how art made a home for itself in Los Angeles. Just as a great work of art forces us to engage with it, redefining our notions of art and art history, *Pacific Standard Time* has us rethink Los Angeles itself as a source inspiration and creativity, as home to postar American art.

September 7, 2011

COMEDY, SERIOUSLY

Can comedy save a life?

A few years ago, Marc Maron, a comic of more than twenty-five years standing, was at his lowest point—rock bottom—ready to give up on everything, even his life. Today, he has a just-released new comedy album, *This Has to Be Funny* (Comedy Central Records), a thriving stand-up career, he's writing an autobiography, recently delivered the keynote address at the Montreal Comedy Festival and has a cult-like following for his podcast—a twice-weekly conversation with comics.

And it is that last, the podcast, that, quite literally, saved his life and has given him a place in the comedy world, along the way creating a community of comedy geeks. WTF? you say. Exactly!

Since Sept. 1, 2009, Maron has created his podcasts, dubbed *WTF,* from his garage (for the most part) where he talks to comics (for the most part). He recently marked his 200th episode. Since launching, Maron says he has garnered more than 20 million downloads, accessible through the Web, his app, or from iTunes, and he's been praised by *Rolling Stone, Vanity Fair, The Onion, Slate* and *The New York Times.*

Maron's parents hail from New Jersey. He, too, was born there, but the family moved to Albuquerque, NM, when he was young. From a very early age, he loved comics and comedy.

"My parents took me to see Jackie Vernon," he recalled in an interview. "I was probably eleven or twelve years old. I wanted to see him; he was one of my favorites." That was his first experience with live comedy.

He always knew he wanted to be a stand-up comic. "It seemed to be a noble profession, where you could speak your mind and make people feel better and get attention—everything I needed and wanted."

During his keynote at the Montreal Comedy Festival, Maron went further: "When I was kid watching comedians on TV and listening to their records, they were the only ones that could make it all seem OK. They seemed to cut through the bull—and disarm fears and horror by being clever and funny. I don't think I could have survived my childhood without watching stand-up comics."

After graduating from Boston University, he took the plunge. Over the next 25 years, Maron took on almost every gig available to a comic, including serving as doorman at a comedy club, doing stand-up in rooms large and small nationwide, going on comedy tours, doing TV pilots, live series, specials for HBO and Comedy Central, auditioning for *Saturday Night Live,* hosting game shows, playing an angry promoter in *Almost Famous,* appearing off-Broadway in his one man show, *The Jerusalem Syndrome* (now available in book form), and doing radio and TV in every format. And yet, until recently, it seemed to be going nowhere.

Shortly after he moved to Los Angeles, after years of living in Astoria, Queens, he got call from Janeane Garafolo, saying, "There's this new thing, Air America." It was to be a new radio station: "It's going to be political. They're looking for comedy." She asked if he was interested, "I said, 'Hell, yeah!' "

"I got in there, and I'd never done anything like that. It was hard work. I learned a lot…It changed my life, definitely," he said. Looking back, he sees his radio education as having "changed my trajectory more than anything else. I don't know if I'd be doing a podcast without that."

As much as he enjoyed radio, the business of Air America was a mess. Maron had already been fired twice when Air America approached him about an Internet TV job, which he accepted only because he was going through a divorce and thought the money would help set him free—but Air America ran out of money first.

Broke, defeated, in danger of losing his LA home—things seemed so bad, he told the audience in Montreal, he found the thought of suicide relaxing.

Although Air America had fired him, they hadn't taken away his entry card to the studio.

"Me and my partner, my producer, we started to do these podcasts, recording them in their studios after hours, and that's how it started."

Maron reached out to friends, other comics, and their conversations were about comedy and their lives. Eventually, the podcasts moved to the garage of his home, where most of them now are recorded. Initially these voice-only interviews may have seemed like a form of self-therapy for Maron, but they eventually also became a safe haven for his guests to talk about their lives, as well.

By now, Maron has interviewed Louis C.K. (a two-parter, where they reviewed and patched up their more than two decades of friendship), Robin Williams, Ben Stiller, Patton Oswalt, Phil Rosenthal, Jeffrey Ross and Garofalo, among many others. Even the normally guarded Conan O'Brien opened up to him.

Perhaps because a podcast is heard, not seen, the conversations sound particularly personal and intimate. In a two-part conversation with Judd Apatow, whom Maron dubbed "the original comedy nerd," they discuss how Apatow, at 16, had a high-school radio program much like what Maron is doing, where Apatow interviewed emerging comics, including Jerry Seinfeld, Jay Leno and Garry Shandling. Maron even played some of those clips, in which you can almost hear Apatow dreaming his future. Apatow spoke candidly, admitting that all his work is about being a guy who's still, at least in his head, a kid who would prefer to stay in his room and watch TV but must learn to connect with his loved ones—his wife, his kids, the world.

In a recent interview with Aubrey Plaza ("Parks and Recreation"), she starts by claiming how easily her career success had come but also shared that, since age 12, she has obsessed about being on *SNL*, and how at 20 she suffered a stroke. All this in a conversation that was as gentle as it was revealing.

For someone whose comedy was once full of bitterness and envy, Maron offers a wonderful quality of gratitude in his interviews—toward the guest for coming, delight at the conversation, and, by episode's end, amazement at what guests as varied as Andrew Dice Clay, Demetri Martin and Shandling have shared. As Maron, who is 12 years sober, put it, "My bitterness is not a choice. The real choice when you're bitter has to be to stop it...I don't think anyone is fundamentally bitter. It comes from disappointment, entitlement and a lot of ego."

Now that he likes what he's doing, Maron finds himself engaged and excited.

Maron is proud to have created a business of his own, and he is trying to extend what he does, by interviewing a greater range of people, by doing live *WTF* shows that tend to be more comedic—funnier—than his interviews, and releasing a new CD, which Maron calls his "best album." And, given that many of the podcast's fans don't know him from his stand-up, they can discover on the CD Maron's riffs on facial hair, including his own (he's against handlebar mustaches), the way he dresses (he's gone from dressing like a college student to dressing like a hip college professor), his trip to the Creation Museum (for all the wrong reasons), dating aggressively, and other reports from his personal frontline. Fundamentally, however, Maron, is grateful for what he's got now—even if his place in the universe is, literally, in his garage.

"I am definitely happy where I am at—I'm incredibly anxious about everything else. I'm not as angry as I was. I definitely feel like I'm contributing something to the world, that I'm engaging my creativity and that I'm being respected for what I do. And that people are coming out to see my stand-up. I'm not a big star, and I don't know if that will ever happen. But I seem to have carved out my own place in this world for myself, and that's a relief, and I'm grateful that it happened, and I'm happy about that."

September 7, 2011

MEL THE AVENGER

In the reaction to the announcement that Mel Gibson was going to make a film about Judah Maccabee, the discussion has focused on whether Gibson should be the one to tell the story of this Jewish hero. I believe the concern should not be so much about whether he is the right person, as what story it is that Gibson is actually going to tell.

Gibson first announced (or threatened, as the case may be) that he was going to make a movie about the Maccabees when Jewish organizations were protesting *The Passion of the Christ.* What Gibson promised was the real story of the Maccabees.

The story of Hannukah may be a heart-warming miracle, but the Maccabees, in truth, were anything but that. One could argue they were the Taliban of their day, religious zealots who put to death those of their fellow Jews they found not to be sufficiently pious.

Despite the romance that has become Masada, and the young soldiers and tourists that are taken there to bond with Jewish glory, the Maccabees essentially organized a death cult, a suicide pact, that we might compare to other modern cults in Jonestown or Waco, and that stand out in marked contrast to Jewish belief, practice and history.

Gibson, over and over again, in his movies, be it *Braveheart* or *The Passion* or *Apocalypto* has put forward a belief that blood and gore, torture and murder lead to transformative, redemptive, even religious experiences. Gibson's Maccabee movie, is to be written by Joe Eszterhas, who after penning *The Music Box* about a daughter who discovers her father was a Nazi collaborator, discovered his own father was a Hungarian Nazi collaborator, and has recently himself, found religion.

Gibson's *Maccabee* could well be his response to his Jewish critics, giving them a dose of Gibson's bloody medicine, payback for their criticism of him, his father (and in Gibson's mind), his religion.

I have no idea whether this movie will ever get made (although Gibson still has enough money to finance it himself). However, if it does, I think it's message will not be of how Jews are a light to the world, but rather a tale of how imperfect their heroes are in fact. Perhaps, in the end, that will be good for the Jews. But I doubt it.

September 7, 2011

WASSERSTEIN & THE LOST BOYS

When the Pulitzer- and Tony Award-winning playwright Wendy Wasserstein—beloved for her plays *The Heidi Chronicles, The Sisters Rosensweig* and *Isn't it Romantic?*—died in 2006 at age fifty-five, Broadway dimmed its lights in her honor. Five years later, Julie Salamon's page-turning biography *Wendy and the Lost Boys* (The Penguin Press: $29.95) sheds light on the public and private selves of this author, whose own family dramas were no less gripping than those she wrote for the stage.

The title's reference to *Peter Pan* is apt on many levels—Wasserstein was named for J. M. Barrie's lost boys' surrogate mother; she also became the chronicler for a generation that didn't want to grow up; and, throughout her life, she surrounded herself with unattainable men, companions whom she could not commit to or who, being gay, were romantically out of reach. When she was 48, Wasserstein chose to become a single mother, and the identity of the father of her child, whose premature birth she chronicled in *The New Yorker,* remains a secret.

Wasserstein's life illustrates the post-immigrant Jewish experience. Her parents' origins were like folklore from a distant past, and their drive to make it in America was manifest in their move up from Brooklyn to Manhattan. For Wasserstein and her peers, assimilation was neither a goal nor a fear—it had already been accomplished. Even though she started her schooling at the Yeshiva of Flatbush, she soon moved to Manhattan's private Calhoun School, then on to Mount Holyoke College in Massachusetts, and, later, City University of New York for graduate work, where she was taught and mentored by Joseph Heller, and finally, to Yale School of Drama, where she earned her M.F.A. degree.

For Wasserstein, who came of age in the "me decade" 1970s, the issue was identity, not religion. No doors were closed because she was Jewish; on the contrary, Wasserstein and her characters suffer from too many options—wondering whether the things they so wished for (careers) were what they really wanted after all (instead of family). The constant refrain in her work is: What was the cost of the trade-offs?

Salamon was given access to Wasserstein's papers and conducted more than 300 interviews with the playwright's friends, family and theater associates. She has done a masterful job of reporting and weaving a narrative portrait of a woman to whom her audience felt such a personal connection that they regularly stopped her on the street to engage her in conversation.

Wasserstein's story is also that of a tight circle of playwrights, directors, producers and actors that included Christopher Durang, Terrence McNally, Andre Bishop, Daniel Sullivan, Meryl Streep and Swoosie Kurtz, and was largely played out at Playwrights Horizon and the Vivian Beaumont Theatre at Lincoln Center.

But there is also her relationship with her notable siblings: Sandra, one of the highest-ranking Fortune 500 executives, for whom there was no glass ceiling; Bruce, the much written-about takeover specialist and billionaire investment banker; and Georgette, who ran an inn in Vermont. All of which was previously known.

However, Salamon reveals what Wasserstein wouldn't: that her two older siblings had a different father, George Wasserstein, who died of an infection following a ruptured appendix. Wasserstein's mother, Lola, then married George's younger brother, Morris, a fact not mentioned to Wasserstein until she was much older. Further, Wasserstein had an older brother, Abner, who had mental deficits and was put in a group home and rarely acknowledged, much less visited, by the family. Lola was the force of nature that Wendy had to deal with, and who provided anecdotal material for friends and in her writing—but it was Lola's secrets that Wasserstein kept off-limits.

I met Wasserstein on a few occasions. She wrote the words for a comic strip that ran in New York Woman when my wife was that magazine's publisher, and so we found ourselves at several of the magazine's events. In my memory, she is a bit like Hagrid in *Harry Potter,* a lovable giant with a wild, thick mane of hair—that is, if Hagrid had appeared at black-tie champagne events. When you talked to Wasserstein, you felt like there was extra oxygen in the air—smiling was inevitable.

After her death, *New York Times* theater critic and columnist Frank Rich wrote: "How could the most public artist in New York keep so much locked up?"

As Salamon makes clear, Wasserstein's friends were her life, and their relationships often turned up transmuted in her work, causing friendships with Wasserstein to run hot and cold. Perhaps Wasserstein compartmentalized her friends and kept her secrets as a means of maintaining a fiction—that they lived in a Neverland of her own invention.

Peter Pan's Wendy refuses the boy's entreaties to stay young, instead maturing until, one day, her own daughter is visited by Peter. In *Wendy and the Lost Boys,* Salamon details the human cost of a life that will live on, on stage, but was cut far too short in real life.

September 14, 2011

A DANIELEWSKI HALLOWEEN

On Halloween this year, instead of being the best sugar pusher in the neighborhood, or following your inappropriately costumed progeny as they amass their candy fortunes, or abandoning your own hard-earned dignity for a night of brew-fueled revelry, let me steer the adults amongst you to REDCAT, the CalArts downtown theater at Walt Disney Concert Hall, where for one night only, Mark Z. Danielewski will conduct a staged reading with shadow puppets and musical accompaniment of his Halloween-set story, *The Fifty Year Sword.* The evening will also raise funds for the Juvenile Diabetes Research Foundation (JDRF) in honor of the son of one of Danielewski's close friends, who was diagnosed with Type 1 diabetes on Halloween.

"*The Fifty Year Sword* is a tale that is told to five orphans," Danielewski, forty-five, explained recently, "and slowly, through the tale, you realize that the orphans are being threatened and that threat is severe enough to curtail their lives. Anyone who is cut by any of the swords will feel that cut in their 50th year…It creates a very specific date, and, on a philosophical level, if you knew you were going to die at this time, it would shape your life. So the idea is, how do you protect those children, and who protects them?"

The performance will feature five actors providing the voices, the 40-foot shadows of shadow-caster Christine Marie, sound design by John Zalewski and music from several original Harry Partch instruments (which is appropriate, as Partch created his own instruments to play a tonal scale of his own invention, much as Danielewski does through his fiction).

Danielewski, author of the experimental novels *House of Leaves* and *Only Revolutions,* has lived in Los Angeles for more than two decades, and this performance at REDCAT is a continuation of his attempts to give meaning to contemporary life by pushing the conventions and traditions of storytelling.

Danielewski was born in New York City. His father, Tad Danielewski, was a Polish-born director and acting teacher who, as a young man, survived the Warsaw uprising only to be sent to a Nazi labor camp before being rescued by the American forces. In the United States, Tad was a director during the golden age of television, directing *Omnibus,* then went on to become a programming executive at NBC who, among his claims to fame, gave Woody Allen his first TV job.

However, when the younger Danielewski was growing up, his father was working on a series of films that had the family moving to far-flung locations, including traveling to Ghana for the Emmy Award-winning series *Africa* and working with Nobel Prize winner Pearl S. Buck on *The Guide,* about India. Danielewski said his parents presented culture as something both accessible and not expensive. "You go to the Prado and look at these amazing paintings, and my Mom would say, 'Draw this.' We would go to the movies, and my father would say, 'Let's talk about how this is a political movie. How is it made?' "

In 1972, his father was making a movie in Spain, *España Puerta Abierta,* on which he had spent two years and his life savings of $2 million, when the film was confiscated by the Franco government. Danielewski's father returned to New York with, literally, nothing to show. This setback led to the greatest dislocation in Danielewski's young life, when his father accepted an offer to become a tenured professor and start a film department at Brigham Young University in Provo, Utah. "That's where I ended up going to high school," Danielewski said. "It would have been a great experience if we were Mormons, but we weren't." he added."

Danielewski says he made many good friends, some of whom he remains close with to this day, but they were not, in his words, "like-minded…They did not have a sense of cultural value."

The result? "I have this advice for parents who want their kids to go to great colleges," he said. "Move them to a place that they deem as hellish. It will motivate them to get out of there. I knew that going to a good university would allow me to get back to a place where people like analyzing movies and reading texts."

Danielewski found all that, and Harold Bloom, at Yale.

Although he never took a course from Bloom, he knew he was among those infected with Bloom's love of literature. Danielewski, who graduated in 1988, majored in English at a time when Yale was swirling in the controversies surrounding deconstructionist literary theory, but Bloom inspired in Danielewski a love of Shakespeare and Wallace Stevens. Danielewski also was drawn to the romanticism of the French poets—Apollinaire and Mallarmé as well as Rimbaud and Verlaine, whom he first learned of through a song on Bob Dylan's *Blood on the Tracks*.

If I dwell on Danielewski's formative intellectual roots, it is because they continue to inform his work. Danielewski said he knew from childhood that he would be a novelist. *House of Leaves,* which Danielewski began when he was twenty-six and published eleven years later, combines every form of literature that interests Danielewski, from the traditional coming-of-age story of a young hipster, to the Hollywood genre films, to academic citations, including footnotes replete with irony; it is a meta-work of the modern age. As Danielewski said by way of analogy: "In the old days, you were going to have one job that was going to last most of your life. Nowadays, kids have three or four jobs and...they're assembling a life." Similarly, Danielewski, who at various times has been a plumber, English teacher and served morning coffee, has assembled not only a life, but a lifework.

He said he sees the Halloween performance of *The Fifty Year Sword* as part of an ongoing effort "to get out of my comfort zone." Dealing with a range of personalities, booking rehearsal studios and reacting to how performers change his words is not his usual form.

Which is why, if you are looking for a different sort of Halloween evening, REDCAT is for you. "The piece is not entirely accessible," he admits. "It's difficult. You have to think about it. There is a very definite meaning there, and it does emerge.

"These are complicated ideas: What is, exactly, forgiveness, what is fate, what holds things together, what cuts things apart?"

So consider it this way: "We're raising money for the JDRF. It's for those people who don't want to have sugar. It's...substantial. So maybe I'm offering apples instead of candy," Danielewski, said, adding with a laugh, "and maybe those apples have razor blades in them."

October 26, 2011

WALLACE BERMAN, THE ALEPH MALE

Art exhibitions take many forms. They can be surveys of a time, place, artist or artistic movement. They may reconsider an artist through a new prism, or appreciate the familiar in a new or different way. All too rare is the exhibition that invites the viewer to share in the joy of discovery, engaging us as confidants in new revelations that suddenly seem self-evident. *Speaking in Tongues: Wallace Berman and Robert Heinecken, 1961-1976,* is just such an exhibition. At the Armory Center for the Arts in Pasadena, the show was co-curated by Claudia Bohn-Spector and Sam Mellon.

Berman is probably best-known for his Verifax collages—made with an early Kodak copier, with which Berman appropriated and assembled images, often showing a hand holding a transistor radio on which an image is displayed. (Today, this device appears to prefigure our current smartphone-iPad-iPhone technology.) The works contain a series of various images, repeated in grid format and are often adorned by Hebrew letters.

Heinecken made his photographic compositions without a camera, using appropriated images. Although the two artists' works are very different, their display here, side by side, grouped around themes of code, gesture and narrative, makes clear the conversation that existed between the two and allows the work of each to seem all the more important, influential and contemporary.

In a recent conversation, Bohn-Spector explained that it was while doing research in the Heinecken archives in Tucson, Ariz., that she and Mellon discovered the connection between the two artists and came upon a way of revealing a hitherto unknown symbiosis between them.

Let me confess my ignorance: Until a few weeks ago, I knew little about Wallace Berman—although it turns out that I had seen one of his important works, *Topanga Seed,* when for a column on the launch of *Pacific Standard Time,* I visited the home of Stanley and Elyse Grinstein, where the work sat at the entryway, a huge boulder covered with Hebrew lettering (it's now on view at the Getty). Although the Pasadena exhibition gives equal importance to both artists, because of Berman's imagery I will focus here more on him.

Grinstein called "Wally" (Berman) the "soul" of California's artistic movement in the late 1960s and early 1970s. Berman is variously referred to as a "guru" to the Beat movement and the "father" of California assemblage art.

Berman was born in Staten Island, NY in 1926. When he was 4, his family moved to Boyle Heights in Los Angeles. He attended Fairfax High School, from which he was expelled in 1943 for gambling (his gambling compulsion was such that one of his early artworks consisted of a poker table complete with cards and chips, hung on a wall as a painting). He served in the Navy during World War II, working with sonar and setting off underwater explosives, an experienced that triggered a breakdown. After the war, Berman attended both the Jepson Art Institute and the Chouinard Art Institute.

In the 1950s, Berman became deeply immersed in jazz and the blues, writing a song for Jimmy Witherspoon and designing album covers. (On the day I visited the Armory exhibit, one of the other attendees was a woman who had been friends with "Wally," as she had called him, and she recalled him taking her to jazz clubs in what was known at the time as South Central Los Angeles, even introducing her to Charlie Parker.) He also became part of the Beat movement, spending the next decade shuttling between San Francisco and Los Angeles creating Semina, a limited-edition art magazine that mixed prose, poetry and art from contributors such as Allen Ginsberg, William Burroughs and Jean Cocteau. In 1961, he returned to Los Angeles, settling in Topanga in 1965.

For the next decade, Berman was part of a vibrant Topanga arts community that included actors, artists and musicians, among them Dean Stockwell, Russ Tamblyn, Dennis Hopper, George Herms and Neil Young (Young's *After The Gold Rush* was originally composed as the soundtrack to a Berman film screenplay). Berman was killed in 1976, the night before his 50th birthday, while riding his motorcycle, the victim of a drunk driver.

Berman's love of the printed word and his appreciation of the spiritual dimension of words and letters was manifest in his study of kabbalah, his use of random Hebrew lettering and words in his art, and his adoption of the Hebrew letter "Aleph" as his own identifying symbol. It is both beautiful and haunting to see those Hebrew letters in Berman's works, on display both at the Armory and at the Getty's *Pacific Standard Time: Cross-currents in LA Painting and Sculpture 1950-1970* survey. The Hebrew attests to the ancient and often indecipherable mystical power of both language and art—at once foreign, scary and familiar.

In the Armory exhibition, curators Bohn-Spector and Mellon included postcards, letters and texts by Berman that offer a sense of his inner life and which, at times, read like Kerouac-style free associations, jazz-like hipster monologues. Berman had a great appreciation for the French Surrealists and Dada, and for the symbolist credo of a derangement of the senses to produce transcendence—which may be the best explanation for his nine-minute experimental film, *Aleph* (completed posthumously by Stan Brakhage), which is being screened at the Armory.

Co-curator Mellon's catalog essay about Berman and Heinecken, *Feeling for the Dude: Brotherhood and Masculinity Creeping Through the Ether,* is a personal essay and discussion of the male idioms that pervade the relationship between these two artists (such as military service, gambling, motorcycles and pornography) and that inform their work.

It is striking that both, in those postwar years in California, were immersed in jazz and Beat, and involved in disassembling and reassembling contemporary culture, making paintings without painting, or photographs without cameras, as well as appropriating images—even those shocking to conventional society (such as admittedly pornographic images)—and refashioning them as art.

This recalls nothing so much as the dialogue between those other dudes, Picasso and Braque, who in an earlier Jazz Age in that Parisian Topanga called Montmartre, also created art of the vulgar and exotic (the African-masked whores of *Les Demoiselles d'Avignon*), as well as assemblages from found objects and collages that included the detritus of their everyday lives—newspapers, menus, images of street performers and musicians. Their inventions of Cubism and the art of collage and assemblage would speak to an entire society coping with modernity and to the artists that followed, including Berman and Heinecken, as would these latter two become influential in their own right, upon artists as varied as Robert Rauschenberg, Cindy Sherman and Jeff Koons.

It is the recognition of this secret language between the artists and the generations that *Speaking in Tongues* allows us to discover in Berman and Heinecken. Berman's work and influence, if not so widely known before, should by virtue of *Pacific Standard Time* become a part of our modern canon. To quote *The Big Lebowski*: "The Dude abides."

November 16, 2011

HAVE A VERY MERRY KLEZMATICS HOLIDAY!

On Dec. 19, as part of their 25th anniversary tour, the Klezmatics will perform at Walt Disney Concert Hall for a Chanukah concert featuring both their well-known and new repertoire. On the program are songs by the legendary folksinger Woody Guthrie—or, as he's known in klezmer circles, American-Yiddish poet Aliza Greenblatt's son-in-law.

The band has just released a double CD, *Live at Town Hall*; Erik Greenberg Anjou's documentary, *The Klezmatics: On Holy Ground,* featuring the band's Town Hall concert, as well as performances in Poland and Hungary, is just out on DVD; and they are also working on a new album. There's much to celebrate.

Klezmer—from which the band took its name—is the joyous, expressive music of the Ashkenazi Jews of Eastern Europe, a sound inspired by Bessarabian Romania, as well as the Roma (Gypsies), and is often played at weddings and other celebrations. Originally purely instrumental, Klezmer is a type of music long admired by people of all faiths and performed in Enlightenment-era European churches centuries before becoming the soundtrack to Yiddish life. Its appeal comes from its unique mix of the seemingly conflicting emotions—comic, plaintive, happy, sad, mournful—while also being transcendental and spiritual. It's an infectious idiom that, like Yiddish itself, is forever being pronounced dead or dying, or dismissed as an artifact of a disappearing Jewish life that, nonetheless, persists in growing and reinventing itself.

The Klezmatics got their start in 1986, when Frank London, who had been playing jazz and rock 'n' roll, placed an ad in the Village Voice looking to start a Klezmer band. Among the respondents was Lorin Sklamberg, a Los Angeles-born, classically trained musician who had a day job at the YIVO Institute for Jewish Research. As Sklamberg recounted recently, he worked on the same floor where the sound archives were located.

"The YIVO sound archives have touched virtually everybody who plays klezmer music," he said, "because it was the first place that people knew of that housed historical recordings of Yiddish music, particularly instrumentals for klezmer music. It's really one of the catalysts of the klezmer music revival. I don't know if the klezmer revival would have been possible without it." Sklamberg was allowed to pore through the recordings and make cassettes of whatever caught his fancy. That was, Sklamberg said, "the band's music education and my own."

Sklamberg still works at YIVO, but today he is "the caretaker of the collection."

"That's very lovely for me," he continued, "because now I know enough to help other people who are looking for material the way we were looking in the early days of the band. So it's a huge privilege and responsibility."

Or as London put it regarding the Klezmatics: "We see ourselves as links in this glorious chain that never stops growing."

Live at Town Hall is about as good an introduction/sampler/greatest hits collection as one can imagine. Tracks include Klezmatics original clarinetist Margot Leverett joining the band on Abraham Ellstein's "Bobe Tanz" from their first record, high-energy romps from *Rhythm & Jews* featuring clarinetist David Krakauer, selections from their collaboration with Tony Kushner for *The Dybbuk*, "Di krenitse" from their collaboration with Chava Alberstein (who is often referred to as the Joan Baez of Israel) and songs from *Brother Moses Smote the Water*, including "Elijah Rock," featuring Joshua Nelson—the Jewish-African-American exponent of Jewish gospel singing. All this, as well as songs from *Wonder Wheel*, the aforementioned Woody Guthrie collection, which won the 2006 Grammy for best contemporary world music—the only Grammy ever awarded to a klezmer or Jewish-music band, as well as its follow-up, *Woody Guthrie's Happy Joyous Hanukkah.*

"It was so much fun to celebrate being together this long as a band, and to do it by getting everyone who has ever played with the band to be up on stage with us," London said. "There was a lot of nachas—pride—out of the whole concert and CD. So much of what happens to the Klezmatics is more just about being out in the world and being available and open," he said.

Some of this openness has led to collaborations with the likes of Itzhak Perlman and Woody Guthrie. "Who would have known?" London said, adding that he could never have foreseen that "Joshua Nelson has turned out to be one of the most enduring and fun collaborations."

Certainly, no one could have predicted the hugely popular music festivals like the Jewish Music Festival in Krakow, Poland, where klezmer is played day and night, performed primarily by non-Jews to mostly non-Jewish audiences in a country that has few Jews.

Sklamberg is philosophical about this turn of events: "It's part of where this music lives now…One of the things you are reminded of when you perform in places like Krakow, is that this is where this music came from." Sometimes these foreign audiences have an immediate and gut reaction to the music that is missing among American Jews who weren't raised with the music or have no connection to Yiddish, he said. "It's funny that the music is heard with different ears and is felt in different ways by different people."

The Klezmatics' documentary is not so much a concert film as it is an *Anvil! The Story of Anvil*-like tale of the band's interpersonal, professional and financial travails, which came as a surprise to London. "If you had polled the band on what they thought the movie would be about, I don't think any one of us would have said that."

In a recent article, *The Wall Street Journal* declaimed: "While the new album marks twenty-five years, those who watch the documentary may wonder if the Klezmatics will make it to 26."

I prefer the see the documentary not so much as the story of a fraying band, but of how, despite the challenges of this digital age, it persists.

It's a matter of endurance, as well. Twenty-five years on, as both London and Sklamberg remarked to me, they still find inspiration in klezmer as their birthright and their heritage, but they also are still discovering ways to make it new. Their show at Disney Hall offers a chance to celebrate all that, and Chanukah, too.

December 7, 2012

ART AND FASHION

Cubes of color intersected by bands, which the viewer can manipulate into arrangements within a grid framing the work; watercolors of narrow striations, punctuated by colors and shapes, transform abstraction from cool cerebral to emotional landscapes. Clothing made in Los Angeles but destined for the world, an ongoing narrative about fabric and color draped over the human form. Such is the work and art of Moshé Elimelech and Shelli Segal, who live with their twin daughters in an ultra-contemporary home in Burbank. Elimelech's work is currently on view in exhibitions at LA Artcore downtown and L2Kontemporary Gallery in Chinatown. Segal is a renown fashion designer.

Elimelech was born in Rabat, Morocco. His Orthodox Jewish parents fled the country and settled in Israel when he was only 2. From an early age, Elimelech took to art, sketching landscapes before turning to oil paints. "It seemed in school that I was always the best in art," said Elimelech.

Although admission to the Avni Institute of Art and Design was meant for those over sixteen, Elimelech lied about his age to get in. At the time, he was still observant, and art school opened his eyes in more ways than one. He recalls his very first class was life drawing, and he's not sure who stared more: he at the nude model or she at his kippah.

Elimelech trained as a designer during his stint in the Israeli army, where he served for two and a half years as art director for the army publication house Maarachot, designing its magazine as well as covers for its books. Following his army service, he worked as the assistant art director for a fashion magazine for about nine months before saving up for a trip abroad.

His first "target," as he put it, was London. He couldn't speak a word of English. His money ran out in three months, after which he took a series of odd jobs, including working "in a supermarket, with cockneys in a factory, and in an Israeli restaurant." When his English improved, he started taking his portfolio around and getting freelance design assignments. Then one day, the phone rang.

It was Israeli artist Yaacov Agam, and he wanted to know if Elimelech could come to Paris immediately to work in his studio. It turned out that one of Agam's assistants, who was a friend of Elimelech's, was leaving and recommended him. Within a few weeks, he was living in Paris and working in Agam's studio. Agam is very particular about his color choices for his work, and in Elimelech he discovered a kindred spirit of sorts; someone whose use and choice of color he came to trust. Still, being a great artist's assistant is its own travail, and once Elimelech had saved enough, he bought a one-way ticket to New York.

In New York, he moved in with an Israeli friend in Brooklyn and took the subway into Manhattan with his portfolio, looking for freelance design work. On New Year's Eve of 1976, he and a friend went to New York's Ocean Club. As the band was playing, he and his friend saw an attractive woman standing nearby.

They flipped a coin to determine who would try talking to her. And that was how Elimelech met his wife, Shelli Segal. "You could say Moshé either won or lost the coin toss, depending on your point of view," Segal joked.

Segal, who was born in Texas, grew up in New York and attended the High School of Music & Art. Although she enjoyed the school, she quickly discovered she wasn't well suited to being on stage. "I wasn't one of those people," she said.

Segal recalled being "an awkward teenager" with one best friend, Charles Busch, who would go on to fame as the playwright/performer of *Vampire Lesbians of Sodom* and *The Tale of the Allergist's Wife*. "He was my only friend," she said.

Segal enrolled at Purchase College, State University of New York, but had to drop out—an assignment using a circular saw resulted in Segal cutting into her fingers (one of which had to be removed).

Instead, Segal enrolled in the Mayer School of Fashion Design, a nine-month New York trade school program in which she learned to make patterns and sew. "After that, I was lucky enough to meet Ruth Manchester, who was a hot designer, and she gave me a job. I was 19, and I've been working ever since," Segal said, adding, "I always knew I wanted to be a designer, not an artist."

After meeting, they lived in New York—Elimelech a graphic designer, Segal a fashion designer. However, Segal's brother, actor Robby Benson, was living in Los Angeles, and Segal's parents, writer Jerry Segal and singer Ann Benson, followed. Suddenly, they felt alone in New York and, in 1981, they decided to move to Los Angeles. "All my New York friends thought I was a nut case," Elimelech said.

Elimelech opened a graphic design studio and continued to work on his art on the side. He was selected as a contributing artist for the 1984 Olympic Games, designing a memorable poster that, in its use of color and striations, prefigures elements of his current work. After working for several LA-based designers, Segal in 1992 became head designer of Laundry, a popular fashion line. "Laundry by Shelli Segal" became a great success and was acquired by Liz Clairborne in 1999.

By 2000, Elimelech decided to close his graphic design studio downtown to devote himself more to his family and his art, at his home studio.

His work is challenging—there is a coolness to the hard-edged graphics and brushed metal frames holding the cubes that resists interpretation. The possible mathematical combinations the work yields by virtue of the multisided cubes and the grid that holds them speak of a certain intellectual rigor, but are, at the same time, whimsical and playful. By contrast, the watercolors, perhaps because they betray more man-made evidence in the lines, grids and the way the colors seep in, are more emotive, suggesting skyscapes and the special light in Los Angeles. Like a beautiful circuit board, the series of lines and line breaks in the watercolors, interrupted by color and taking various forms, sometimes reveal patterns in the work that reorganize what we are looking at, as if to decode a secret message whose truth is more sensory than intellectual.

If all this seems like a contradiction, it perfectly suits Elimelech and Segal, a New York couple who are very much settled in Burbank; whose work could be done anywhere but speaks of Los Angeles; and who have excelled in creative pursuits while leading a very non-Hollywood life. Yet one could argue that they are both, by virtue of what they design, in the "show" business. Imagine that.

February 1, 2012

LOOKING AT THE CLOUD FROM BOTH SIDES NOW

I listen to music all day, in my car, in my office, at the gym, while walking the dog or taking a hike. Most of what I listen to I don't have to pay for; some of it I do. There are so many ways to discover new music or find old favorites that I thought it might be useful to create a guide to the various offerings—on the cloud, the Net or on the air—these days, based on my personal experience, thus far.

Terrestrial radio

Old-school radio, AM or FM, still works fine and is still free, and when my teenage daughter is in the car, we ping-pong among the hit-driven radio stations 97.1 KAMP-FM (Amp Radio), 102.7 KIIS-FM (Kiss FM) and 105.9 FM Los Angeles (POWER 106), until the ads take over all the stations—seemingly simultaneously. And while the music on 89.9 KCRW-FM is not interrupted by ads, the station does have pledge drives.

Nonetheless, most mornings I listen to KCRW's "Morning Becomes Eclectic" from 9:00 a.m. to noon. This show, where I discover most of my favorite new music, is best described as "adult alternative" and "world music," and features mostly singer-songwriters and their bands, including some live performances and interviews. And on weekends, if allowed the pleasure, I try to listen to part of "Nothin' but the Blues," which airs on 88.1 FM KJAZZ from 2:00 to 7:00 p.m. on weekends.

Cloud-based music lockers

One of the reasons I don't need to play my CDs anymore, or even my iPod, is because I've uploaded much of my music onto the Web. Google offers a music service that allows you to store a great deal of music for free. Apple, too, has just launched iCloud, which will copy music in the formats it recognizes to a (thus far) free locker. In addition, for twenty-five dollars a year, its "music match" program will upload all your music to the cloud. With these services, you can access your music on multiple home, personal and mobile devices. Spotify (which I'll discuss later in greater detail) also allows you to upload your music, but you can only access that music for free on your computer.

Internet radio and streaming music services (Pandora and Spotify)

If you sign onto iTunes and click on "radio," you will be able to access a wide selection of radio stations from all over the country. However, not all stations travel well. I tried both WFMU, the Fordham University radio station in New York, where many of the DJs of my youth now toil, as well as WWOZ, New Orleans' legendary music station, and I found that, much like Café Du Monde beignets, they are much better consumed right on site.

Pandora and Spotify are the two most popular music-streaming services (others include MOG, Yahoo music, Rdio and Last.fm), and the differences between them are as much generational as feature-driven. If you grew up on FM radio and like to be surprised (pleasantly) by music you enjoy, Pandora will appeal to you. Pandora allows you to create "channels" or music streams by artist or song, and then brings you complementary music. Your musical choices can be mainstream or obscure (I have a Professor Longhair channel), and it allows you to mix any of the streams you establish. It works with the same kind of algorithms that Netflix uses, basing its offerings on your previous choices. So, for example, if you create a Rolling Stones or Bonnie Raitt channel, you might be delighted, as I was, suddenly to hear an eighteen-minute version of "I Heard It Through the Grapevine" performed by Creedence Clearwater Revival.

On the other hand, if you came of age in the mix-tape or playlist-driven era, Spotify might be your preference, as it allows you to upload your own music, create playlists and play any song that is in its capacious library. You can also share your playlists or songs with friends. Spotify is where I go when I know what I want to hear, say, the new Bangles record, *Sweetheart of the Sun*. Spotify recently teamed up with Rolling Stone magazine to allow subscribers of both to import all the celebrity playlists from their "playlist issue," such as "Mike D's Top Classic New York Hip-Hop" or "Jimmy Cliff's Top Lost Reggae Classics." Spotify also has just teamed up with Facebook to allow you to share music with friends and to be able to see what playlists your friends are listening to on Spotify (which may be the killer app).

Satellite radio

It is, as I prefer to think of it, crack for new car owners. These days most cars come with free-trial satellite radio. Once you've tried it, it's hard to give up—conversion rates hover around 50 percent, according to a Sirius executive. There are now more than 21 million subscribers. The cost is anywhere from $9 to $17 a month, plus tax; although you can instead get an Internet subscription for $4 a month and play it on your smartphone through your car. Satellite is, for the most part, commercial free, and the menu of offerings is vast, with channels devoted to decades ('60s, '70s, '80s, '90s), genres and subgenres (country, bluegrass, blues, jazz, metal, rock, folk), performers and bands (Springsteen, Jimmy Buffett, Dave Matthews, Willie Nelson), custom compilations, with names like The Spectrum, The Blend, The Loft, Coffeehouse and, of course, The Joint (a reggae station). What stations you listen to could soon become a pick-up line, akin to the 1970s-era catch all, "What's your sign?"

There is one other reason that many people can't resist satellite, and its name is "Howard." When Howard Stern departed terrestrial radio, those of us who didn't follow him to paid radio may have thought that his moment of cultural relevance had ended. Yet satellite, its own parallel universe, reveals that Howard is still in his glory—some argue he's better than ever. Listening to Howard, like playing golf or surfing, is all about waiting for that one unparalleled moment or experience. No one does interviews like Howard—the questions he asks and the answers he elicits are part of why he's so addictive.

It may not all be all heavenly, but, to quote Joni Mitchell, "I've looked at clouds from both sides now." And, free or paid, that's where I now go to stream her music.

March 7, 2012

DEMJANJUK'S JUST EPITAPH

The recent death of John Demjanjuk, ninety-one, in a nursing home in Germany, brings to a close one of the most extensive and most contested Nazi war crimes prosecutions in history, a process that began in the United States in the mid 1970s and was ongoing at the time of his death as Demjanjuk awaited the appeal of his conviction in Germany as an accessory to the more than 28,000 murders of Jewish men, women and children committed during the time he served as a camp guard at the Sobibor extermination camp.

In the immediate aftermath of his death there will be those, no doubt, who will argue that he was an innocent or at best served under duress, or at worst was a mere cog in the machine. There will be those who would repeat the canards expressed throughout his more than thirty years of prosecution in the United States, Israel and Germany, that the damning documents that prove his Nazi service were fakes and KGB forgeries, even though every court at every stage that has examined the documents has found them authentic and consistent with each other, proving that Demjanjuk was the bearer of Nazi identification card No. 1393, issued at the Trawniki training camp, that lists and correlates his Nazi service not only at Trawniki and

Sobibor but also subsequently at the Flossenburg and Majdanek camps. There will be those who argue against the trying of old men, against the waste of resources, the time, the money, the prosecutorial effort.

There also will be many who, having no argument with Demjanjuk's prosecution or conviction, will still, in the face of Demjanjuk's long life and the thought of him spending his final days in a nursing home in Germany, ask: Was justice done?

As someone who spent many months in the Jerusalem courtroom attending the trial of Demjanjuk and followed closely every stage of his American and German proceedings, I would argue that, to borrow a biblical phrase, not only was justice done, it was seen to be done.

The notion that Demjanjuk, awaiting the appeal of his German conviction, living in a nursing home, was "free" is to ignore the reality of his existence—confined in a foreign country, cut off from family, friends and community, left to die with the mark of Cain upon him. The fact that almost every article concerning his death contained the words "convicted Nazi camp guard" is only one small measure of history's judgment and of justice being done.

Demjanjuk's prosecutions have added greatly to our knowledge of how the Final Solution, the unfathomable murder of millions, was carried out by the unexceptional—and not only by the Germans but also by their willing collaborators and henchmen. The death camps were commanded by Germans and staffed by their auxiliary guards, such as Demjanjuk, without whom the murders could not have been accomplished.

Despite the fact that Demjanjuk denied any and all involvement in the crimes of the Holocaust, he was demonstrated to be an exceptionally bad liar whose own accounts of his whereabouts were riddled with inconsistencies, impossibilities, untruths and evasions that bordered on admissions. The record by now is all too clear: Born in Soviet Ukraine, he was a Red Army soldier captured by the Germans who volunteered to serve the Nazis. Trained at Trawniki, and issued his Nazi ID there, he became an experienced camp guard serving at labor, concentration and extermination camps whose only function was the expeditious murder of innocent civilian Jewish men, women and children. He may have also served in the pro-Nazi Vlaslov Army both by his own admission and by reason of a Nazi blood group tattoo that he tried to erase. All of which, even any of which, had Demjanjuk revealed when he applied to or entered the United States would have been sufficient cause to deny him admission and bar him from citizenship, and which were cause for his denaturalization and deportation.

Those murdered at Sobibor and the other camps where Demjanjuk served cannot cry out for justice. There are no graves, other than the mass graves where they were killed, at which to mourn them. It is easy to imagine that those who committed the crimes thought no one would ever know who the perpetrators were or, worse, that no one would care. Perhaps they imagined that they could, like Demjanjuk, deny everything. Who would prosecute them? What could they prove? It is to the everlasting credit of the United States, Israel and Germany that over the last three decades they continued to prosecute the guilty, not only the planners, the officials or the commandants but also the guards and policemen; not only the desktop murderers but also those with blood on their hands.

The generation that saw the Nazi horrors firsthand will soon pass from this world. Demjanjuk's trial may well be the last major Nazi war crimes trial. If so, then Demjanjuk's epitaph is just: not that he died a free man but that he died, in the eyes of the world and for all history that follows, a convicted Nazi war camp guard.

March 22, 2012

JONATHAN FOER'S *NEW AMERICAN HAGGADAH*

EXTREMELY UNSURPRISING AND INCREDIBLY SIMILAR

The haggadah, the user's manual to the Passover seder, might be the world's oldest annually practiced ritual, and the story of the Jews' freedom from slavery in Egypt is, Jonathan Safran Foer said recently, "the best-known greatest continuously read story" in book form. And yet, just like there isn't a singer who doesn't think he can cover a Bob Dylan song better than Dylan himself, the haggadah remains the book that everyone thinks they can improve on.

The *Maxwell House Haggadah* might be good enough for the White House, but at homes across the country there are any number of printed and self-stapled versions, including egalitarian, feminist and vegan versions with prayers writ special for women, children, Russian Jews, Ethiopian Jews, and for the liberation of a wide variety of groups and causes, even those without benefit of 501(c)(3) tax-exempt charitable status. At our seders, the reading has been interrupted for comic plays, showings of Charlton Heston parting the Red Sea, and after-dinner rounds of comic songs, including the much-maligned version of "Brisket," sung to the tune of The Association's "Windy."

In other words, there is a good case to be made that we need a *New American Haggadah* (Little, Brown and Co.: $29.99). As luck would have it, one has just been published, edited and with an introduction by novelist and anthologist Jonathan Safran Foer, as well as translation from the Hebrew by Nathan Englander, novelist and, not incidentally, a graduate of the Hebrew Academy of Nassau County.

As Foer explained recently at a Writers Bloc event in Beverly Hills, every detail was considered in this haggadah's nine-year gestation period. That the book lies flat—no accident. That it is of a certain size, to take importance on the table but not to crowd your neighbor—done on purpose. No representational art (despite a commissioned but never-used work by R.B. Kitaj)—a decision made because the visuals might detract from the text. More money spent on contributions made and killed than on those appearing in the book—true. As Foer explained, the process of allowing the *New American Haggadah* to take the form took time, and the final result, much to Foer's surprise, was more traditional than he would ever have imagined.

Similarly, Englander calls his translation "hyper-literal." Englander adds a grace to the translation not usually evident, as well as moments of subtle poetry, as when he translates what is usually read as "Our Lord, God" instead as "Lord, God-of-Us." The strength of Englander's translation is, in some ways, its greatest weakness—it demands a more complete reading and a little more stamina and does not easily accommodate the fast-forward skipping and speed-reading of the haggadah that many have embraced as part of the tradition.

Alas, I truly wish I were more excited by this *New American Haggadah* Foer is clearly a very thoughtful, intelligent person. His novels, such as *Everything Is Illuminated* and *Extremely Loud and Incredibly Close,* brim with inventiveness. There is something scholarly about him, and he harbors a genuine desire to create community, whether it be among a group of writers opining on the work of Joseph Cornell, non-meatarians or his fellow Hebrews. On the face of it, then, he seems a brilliant choice to commission and compile a *New American Haggadah* However, the result is neither new nor particularly American—it is as if Foer wrestled with the haggadah, like Jacob wrestled with the angel, and the haggadah won, repeatedly. To cite but one example: When it came time to name the book, possibilities abounded (i.e. why not *The Brooklyn Haggadah* in honor of where Foer lives), but the final choice *New American Haggadah* although literally correct, is strangely bland.

Or let me put it another way: Imagine you had an old house that had been in the family for many generations—that you thought could, in so many ways, be improved upon. So you consulted the best architects and designers and you took the house apart, tore it down and started over. At each crossroads, when faced with a choice between the suggestions and the original, you found yourself, much to your surprise, siding with the original. In the end, when the house was rebuilt, your friends expressed surprise, saying: "Where's the new house? This is the old house." Not much different and no more serviceable than the original (and in the case of this haggadah, perhaps less usable as it contains no transliteration for those for whom the mumbling of ancient words is incantatory).

I don't want to give the impression that this *New American Haggadah* is not without its pleasures. The commentary is intelligent (Rebecca Newberger Goldstein on Spinoza's seat at the table), tough (Jeffrey Goldberg on the Tenth Plague), learned (Nathaniel Deutsch on Exodus' most theologically shocking moment) and at times subversive (Daniel Handler, aka Lemony Snicket, on the four types of parents). It runs at a 90-degree angle to the Hebrew—and offers not so much exegesis as discussion points for seder attendees. Although the commentary is at times engaging, entertaining and thought provoking, there is never as much of any of those as one might have expected or wanted. There is a timeline across the top of the book that is worth reading, and the graphic design of the pages reflecting the Hebrew typography of each time period is beautiful in its own way; but, again, none of it matches the drama of the story being told. Which, according to Foer, is the point. The story, the text, comes first.

Without the haggadah, the seder is merely a Jewish Thanksgiving dinner whose emphasis is less on ritual than on family, more about side dishes than the main event, more about the heavy meal and the four glasses of wine than the time-bending empathetic command to feel as if we, ourselves, were slaves in Egypt.

Although the *New American Haggadah* may create a whole new gift category—the seder present, thereby selling many copies—my prediction is that few will use it instead of the family haggadah. More likely, this haggadah will be used as a supplement—a reading from Lemony Snicket here, a passage read aloud there—and will become yet another prop in the customization of the seder. Which is, in and of itself, part of the long tradition of haggadahs and Passover seders.

As for us, this year we're ditching the comic play, opting instead for "Passover Jeopardy." Our seder hosts will be overjoyed, no doubt, to receive their copy of the *New American Haggadah* I may even read from it in between the Hebrew and the Maxwell House versions. More likely, I'll be saying: "Pass the charoset, I'll take Moses for $400."

March 29, 2012

CULTURE WITH A SIDE OF POPCORN

When the hit comedy *One Man, Two Guvnors* comes to Broadway this spring, I'll be able to say I saw the London production. I also saw the Metropolitan Opera's new production of *Don Giovanni* with the Polish tenor Mariusz Kwiecien. As for bragging rights, it's hard to match having seen David Hallberg's debut with the Bolshoi Ballet in Moscow in *Sleeping Beauty.* All this, without ever leaving Los Angeles.

I've taken to attending theater, opera and ballet performances from around the world, recorded live in HD and shown in Los Angeles movie theaters, each for less than $20 a ticket, an exceptional value.

My adventures in high culture with a side of popcorn began much like Phileas Fogg's journey, with a performance in London. No sooner had I read a review of Helen Mirren's appearance in the National Theatre's London production of *Phedre,* Racine's great tragedy, than I discovered that it would soon be shown in HD at the Mann Chinese 6 in Hollywood.

Although a screen can't convey the intensity of a live performance, where you feel as if the outside world has stopped as you witness a greater truth revealed, watching *Phedre* it nevertheless felt a privilege to see a world-class performance. Moreover, there were some real benefits that went beyond the availability of concession snacks—no need to feel bad about slouching in your chair or not dressing up, no guilt for getting up midperformance for a bathroom break and no compunction about leaving early. Plus, the advances in HD cinematography are such that, regardless of where I sat, it was like having the best seat in the house.

Over the course of the past year, I've attended two National Theatre performances: the very enjoyable Victorian comedy *London Assurance,* which featured brilliant performances by Simon Russell Beale and Fiona Shaw, and the aforementioned *One Man, Two Guvnors,* whose comic set pieces had the whole audience laughing as one. Upcoming in 2012 for the National Theatre, at UCLA's James Bridges Theater, are the Oliver Goldsmith classic, *She Stoops to Conquer* on April 29, and the acclaimed Danny Boyle-directed production of *Frankenstein,* in June.

As for opera, I had always been told that it was a pleasure I would come to appreciate late in life. My parents were opera goers. I recall with great fondness how my mother would always remark on how, the minute the opera began, my father would fall asleep, only to snap awake when the curtain fell. When I asked him once why he was willing to spend so much on opera tickets if he was going to sleep through the performance, he answered: "Sleep like that I don't get at home!"

I am here to report that after attending *The Met: Live in HD* performance of *Don Giovanni,* not only did I not fall asleep, but for the first time I "got" opera. I realized that Mozart's genius was to take the beautiful sounds of sacred music, associated with the church and heavenly pursuits, and put them in the service of the profane—in *Don Giovanni* there is even an aria where a young woman pleads with her husband to beat her so that they can have makeup sex. *Don Giovanni* is the story of a rake meant as a wake-up call to the 1 percent of its day after the revolutions in America and those about to erupt in France. The closest analogy to contemporary music is the revolutionary way in which Ray Charles, Sam Cooke and Aretha Franklin took the sounds of gospel music and formed "soul music" to narrate the songs of unhallowed human experience and the way in which James Brown made it political.

Opera in HD is a global phenomenon: In addition to the Met's performances, Emerging Pictures "Opera in Cinema" program offers HD performances from La Scala in Milan, the Royal Opera House in London, even from the Liceu in Lisbon.

Given the even greater price differential between live opera and HD, and the similarly large gap in informality, not to mention what I save on plane tickets, I've decided that I'm just as happy to attend the opera in HD in Santa Monica. It's hard to imagine sitting in an opera house eating peanut M&Ms without incurring the daggers of dirty looks all around.

Finally, the Emerging Pictures folk also have a "Ballet in Cinema" program that delivers dance performances from the Bolshoi in Moscow and London's Royal Court. Of the three experiences in HD—theater, opera, ballet—I would say ballet was the least successful.

Watching ballet is often about suspension of disbelief, watching how dancers achieve with ease the hard-to-believe perfection of line, grace of movement, physical prowess and stamina, displaying supra-normal abilities to stand en pointe, leap, lift and turn. On film, our eyes have been trained by the tricks of special effects to accept and even expect the superhuman (think of those flying martial arts scenes in *Crouching Tiger, Hidden Dragon*), and because of this, in ballet on film, the extraordinary seems more ordinary than it should.

My objections aside, it is still mind-boggling to see the Bolshoi dancers perform on their stage in Moscow. Bolshoi means "large" in Russian, but also "grand," and to see a Russian heirloom production such as *Sleeping Beauty,* with music by Tchaikovsky, based on the original choreography by Marius Petipa as passed down to Bolshoi ballet master Yuri Grigorovich, with its seemingly endless depth of dancers, incredible costumes and amazing sets in that storied theater—that is certainly grand—and good value.

Now, a caveat about the theaters—not all are created equal. For example, the sound and the screen at the AMC in Santa Monica, where *The Met: Live in HD* is screened, is not as good as that in Century City (but Century City often sells out). As for the audience at the performances I attended, the crowd was not so much hip as candidates for hip replacement. But so what? There is an easy camaraderie at these performances, where people applaud at will and schmooze during the intermission, trading insider gossip. It's fun (although the more precise technical term would be gemutlich).

One could do worse than to abide by these resolutions: Be lazy. Stay local. Be frugal—see theater, opera and ballet in HD. A world of high culture awaits—a chance to travel the world without ever leaving home, to see great performances in grand locations, at affordable prices with popcorn, candy and soda, as close as a nearby movie theater.

April 11, 2012

CAPTURING THE MUSIC SCENE

The recent regional extravaganza known as Pacific Standard Time (PST), a six-month, far-ranging agglomeration of Southern California exhibitions, installations and performances, began with a series of shows that made a very convincing argument for the importance of art created in Los Angeles from 1945 to 1980.

The role Los Angeles has played in shaping American culture (and, conversely, the role culture has played in shaping LA) was hardly limited to the visual arts, as has been made clear by two exhibitions here: *Trouble in Paradise: Music and Los Angeles 1945-1975,* which just closed at the Grammy Museum at LA LIVE, downtown; and *Who Shot Rock & Roll* at the Annenberg Center for Photography in Century City, which opens June 23 and runs through October 7.

Trouble in Paradise, guest curated by USC professor (and Tommywood alum) Josh Kun was, like its subject of music in California, much more substantial than first appeared. Occupying a small corner of the fourth-floor installation at the Grammy Museum and consisting of a few vitrines of artifacts and a wall or two of information cards along with a timeline, it was a testament to the power of multimedia presentation that the show was able to cover so much territory in depth in such little space.

After World War II, Los Angeles' population surged as a result of the postwar boom, as well as with increased Mexican-American immigration, African-American migration from the South and the many returning vets who decided to settle in California. However, as the city grew, two separate events enforced de facto racial segregation: a new freeway system, which isolated communities rather than uniting them, and the 1950 appointment of William H. Parker III as chief of the Los Angeles Police Department (LAPD), a man intent on keeping Los Angeles, to paraphrase the words of a song by Parliament, "a chocolate city with vanilla suburbs."

Although "California music" generally conjures Beach Boys surf songs, Laurel Canyon-inspired hippie paeans and the Doors playing the Sunset Strip, each with lyrics bemoaning their respective white-people-problems, curator Kun reminded us of the richness and complexity of the region's storied musical history of integration and cross-pollination, be it from the be-bop of Central Avenue, to Ritchie Valens (born Valenzuela)—the self-proclaimed "Little Richard of the Valley"—from *The Nat 'King' Cole Show* on NBC to Marilyn Monroe insisting that the Mocambo nightclub book Ella Fitzgerald, to the legendary T.A.M.I. Show at the Santa Monica Civic Auditorium, directed by Steve Binder and featuring James Brown and the Rolling Stones.

Trouble in Paradise, did an excellent job of excavating such nearly forgotten musical heralds as Hadda Brooks, a singer and pianist who was the first African-American woman to host a TV music and interview program (move over, Oprah!), and

Johnny Otis, the musician, bandleader, impresario and TV host, a Greek immigrant who adopted black Los Angeles. "As a kid," Otis once said, he decided that "if our society said we had to be black or white, [then] I would be black."

It is striking how much landmark music that we don't necessarily associate with Los Angeles was recorded here, from Sam Cooke's "A Change Is Gonna to Come" to James Brown's "Say It Loud—I'm Black and I'm Proud."

Finally, the exhibition also made a convincing display of how much the repressive reign of Chief Parker's LAPD led to epic conflagrations in the African-American community during 1965's Watts Riots (thousands arrested, millions of dollars in damage, 34 dead), in the Mexican-American community during the 1970 Chicano Moratorium rally in Laguna Park to protest the Vietnam War, and among the teenage fans of rock 'n' roll during the 1966 riots on the Sunset Strip protesting curfew laws—all of which also produced memorable music—whether it was Wattstax, the all-day festival of African-American pride held at the Los Angeles Coliseum and immortalized on film, or the music of El Chicano or the Buffalo Springfield's "For What It's Worth."

Like the famous Magritte-inspired cover of Jackson's Browne's 1974 album *Late for the Sky,* California may look sunny from afar, but *Trouble in Paradise,* documented an underlying darkness. Or, to quote, as Kun does, Browne's lyrics from "Before the Deluge," Los Angeles is filled with "the resignation that living brings."

Who Shot Rock & Roll, at the Annenberg Space for Photography, is a group show originally curated for the Brooklyn Museum by author Gail Buckland. It features 166 images, many of them iconic photographs of music legends from the Beatles to Tupac, from Tina Turner to Amy Winehouse, by a wide range of photographers, among them Annie Leibovitz, Henry Diltz, Diane Arbus, Lynn Goldsmith, Bob Gruen, Amy Arbus, Linda McCartney, Albert Watson and many others. It also displays a selection of visually striking music videos, including ones of Elvis Presley, U2, Grace Jones and Sonic Youth, as well as a documentary, commissioned by the Annenberg, that highlights the photographers and their images, incorporating behind-the-scenes footage as well.

There is a vitality to these documents of the music world that seems very Los Angeles. And beyond that, the *Rock & Roll* images captivate on many levels: There's the thrill of seeing an artist in an unguarded moment; of capturing the excitement and energy of performance—a stop-motion documentary of musical self-actualization; but there are also some elaborately staged portraits that, at their best, reveal a larger truth about artist or society at that moment in time. Each genre is very well represented.

In conjunction with the exhibition, the Annenberg is partnering with KCRW (89.9 FM and KCRW.com) for a series of live concerts in July (admission is free, but reservations, at kcrw.com, are suggested). These will feature an acoustic and DJ set by Moby, a T. Rex tribute by Portugal. The Man, and Raphael Saadiq and others performing songs from *Chimes of Freedom,* the Amnesty International benefit collection of Bob Dylan covers.

Trouble in Paradise and *Who Shot Rock & Roll* serve to remind of us of how much music can shape the very landscape of our lives and our times, through journeys that both define and transcend the place where we live.

June 13, 2012

TRUTH, BEAUTY AND DESIRE

Gustav Klimt is best known for his famous golden paintings, portraits of society women adorned in jewels and cloaked in gold, and for the flat two-dimensionality of his work that led many to declare it superficial and merely decorative. The Getty exhibition *Gustav Klimt: The Magic of Line* puts a lie to that characterization, demonstrating how Klimt's work conveys complex emotions and even allegorical ideals.

The Getty's show features more than 100 drawings from throughout the Austrian painter's career— a few from the Getty's own collection, but the majority on loan from the Albertina Museum in Vienna in conjunction with the celebration of the 150th anniversary of Klimt's birth. The exhibition runs until Sept. 23.

"I thought I knew Klimt, but I didn't," said Marian Bisanz-Prakken, curator at the Albertina and the reigning expert on Klimt drawings, discussing what surprised her most about the exhibition. "He was an artist who goes into the elemental situations of life. The cycle of life is presented in a modern approach, a new approach. He brings his subjects to life, and it touches the viewer with immediacy."

The exhibition is chronological and reveals Klimt's early talent at rendering scenes and people with a facility many artists never achieve. As an adult, Klimt drew from live models almost daily. It is amazing to see how he used his natural gifts, at first academically and then with precision, and as he matured, how his drawings became the laboratory where he studied human perspective and tested different approaches for his large-scale portraits. It was also where he expressed the inner yearnings of his subjects.

Klimt had a budding career of large public commissions, such as the frieze to honor Beethoven's Ninth Symphony (a facsimile of which has been installed at the Getty for this exhibition), and as president of the Vienna Secession arts movement he had a great say in the décor of its building headquarters. However, when commissioned to create paintings for the University of Vienna's Great Hall—the university was hoping for historic, allegorical or heroic depictions of law and medicine, for example—Klimt, who had come to believe that true progress for mankind was a chimera and that man was destined to an endless cycle of suffering, war and death, painted works of such nihilism that the university rejected them. In response, Klimt withdrew from public engagement and turned his focus increasingly to portraits.

The Getty exhibition is called "the magic of line" because of Klimt's uncanny ability to render his models as living, breathing creatures while conveying emotion and, in his later work, to explore the vanishing point where desire, eroticism and dreams meet.

Picasso's late work is well known for its erotic content, but it appears in his signature style—it is more about content than form. In Klimt's case, his late drawings, intensely intimate and erotic, represent a new mode of interpretation—his lines change, they become choppy, frenzied almost—as if Klimt is trying to capture a chrysalis in the process of transformation.

Bisanz-Prakken spoke of Klimt's "respect for Eros," while Klimt, who rarely commented on his work, did favor the epigram *Nudas Veritas*—in nakedness is found truth. This begs the question: What truth was Klimt actually looking to find in his drawings of women floating, in a dream state, or lost in the throes of autoeroticism? Though there is no sure answer, there are clues to be found in the particular milieu of the society that surrounded Klimt, his subjects and patrons in Vienna at the start of the 20th century.

In the mid-19th century, Vienna had torn down its medieval city walls and built the Ringstrasse, a circular road that centralized the city's governmental structures along with its cultural institutions and the homes of its wealthiest citizens. Largely financed by Jewish families, the Ringstrasse also became a symbol of the Jewish middle and upper-middle classes' arrival in Austrian society. By the turn of the century, Vienna was in many respects a city dominated by highly cultured, highly assimilated Jews in most walks of life. This was the Vienna of Sigmund Freud, Ludwig Wittgenstein and Arthur Schnitzler, of Karl Kraus and Theodor Herzl.

Klimt was not Jewish, but many of his patrons were (among them Wittgenstein's sister), as were his portrait subjects and models, some of who were believed to also be his lovers. As Klimt drew his highly intimate works of women in an erotic dream state, Freud was treating women from the same social milieu for hysteria and developing psychoanalysis from the interpretation of their dreams; while Schnitzler, with whom Freud corresponded, was writing his stories of sexual dalliances known as *Reigen,* or more popularly as the basis for the Max Ophuls film *La Ronde.* Schnitzler's novella about an erotic dream state, *Traumnovelle,* would be the basis for Stanley Kubrick's *Eyes Wide Shut.*

Perhaps the newly wealthy Viennese Jewish upper-middle class experienced too much freedom in which to explore sex, drugs (Freud was a cocaine evangelist) and Wagnerian music. Regardless, Klimt's drawings are themselves indications and portents of the ferment Vienna would yield.

In Klimt's drawing, these dark-haired Jewesses are the objects of desire, the temptresses, but they are also "the other." They are desired and often beyond reach. The sexual desires, actual and fantasized, among Vienna's Jews, whom Schnitzler chronicled and Freud made a science of, would also be cause for critics such as Karl Kraus to call the age corrupt and without morals. Wittgenstein would champion a movement of "pure" philosophy. This backlash against the rising Jewish middle class in Vienna would also find expression in virulent anti-Semitism.

Freud would forever recall his father being called "Dirty Jew" and having his hat knocked off his head, and Herzl, for his part, would conclude that anti-Semitism was so entrenched, so impossible to combat, that the only solution was to found a Jewish state. At the same time, the desire for truth and beauty found in nature and the healthy expression of sex, as idealized in Klimt's work, would also find its most perverted expression in the tenets of Nazi ideology as promulgated by that Austrian would-be painter, Adolf Hitler. Moreover, the same pseudoscience underlying Hitler's veneration of nature would be used to condemn Jews as "unclean" and characterize the Jewish people as demonic. Freud is often cited as saying, "Sometimes a cigar is just a cigar," but for Klimt, a drawing was more than a collection of lines—it was the portrait of his age's unconscious yearnings and of a Jewish society that the 20th century would mark as indelibly as the magic of a line on a paper.

July 11. 2012

THE PERPETUAL (ONLINE) STUDENT

It seems like only yesterday that my friend Teri was telling me that if she could do college all over again she would take different courses: literature, poetry and just a greater variety of subjects. Well, I've got some good news: turns out that you can now take an amazing variety of courses, many of them offered by universities that most of us couldn't get into today, such as Harvard, Oxford and Stanford, many of them free. What's the hitch? Just this: the courses are online.

I've been taking outside education for most of my life. Just as soon as I started first grade, I started going to Sunday school (which in my case was Tuesday, Thursday and Sunday school); during high school I took life drawing classes at the Art Students League (my only shot at seeing naked people); during college, I also attended summer school (it was how I convinced my parents to first let me drive to California); and after graduate school, I continued to take various creative writing classes.

There came a point, however, when with wife and daughter a priority, I stopped going to classes. Instead, I discovered The Teaching Company, which offers great courses from great professors in a variety of audio and video formats at reasonable prices (there are always sales). Over the years, I have enjoyed

"How to Listen to and Understand Great Music," on cassette; "American Civil War" on CD; and "The Aeneid of Virgil" as a download. I can say that in twenty-minute bursts (the limit of my attention span, not the lectures, which are generally in one-hour installments) a course makes driving around a parking lot looking for a space or being stuck in traffic almost painless.

My father, who footed the bill for my formal education, had an abiding fear that I would become "Der Ewige Student," the perpetual student, never launched into the real world; jack of all trades, master of none. Today, however, it turns out that to remain competitive in the real world, one must continue to learn.

Whatever your profession, there are online courses to get up to speed on new developments and new technologies. So, for example, from mediabistro.com, a source for the media-related industries, I recently took a short workshop in CMS (Content Management Strategy), or how to use WordPress, Drupal and other online platforms. I am considering taking another in Google Analytics or a social media boot camp, not so much to master the specifics but to gain better fluency and increase my comfort level in discussing online media strategies.

At the same time, universities around the world are taking their courses online in ways that may disrupt our notions of how and what we learn, who learns what, what we pay for education and even the value of a specific college degree. More than a year ago, when Sebastian Thrun of Stanford put one of its artificial intelligence courses online for free, 160,000 thousand students from almost 200 countries signed up. Not long thereafter, Coursera was founded by Stanford computer scientists Andrew Ng and Daphne Koller, to offer courses from Stanford, Penn, Michigan and Princeton, and raised more than $20 million in financing. According to *The New York Times*, Harvard and MIT have formed a similar joint venture called EdX, Thrun has launched Udacity, and 2tor has partnered with divisions of USC, Georgetown and UNC to offer online courses. You can sign up for any of these to see what courses they offer. Apple, of course, has an app for that: iTunes U from which you can search and then watch and/or listen to a wide variety of course offerings.

What are some of the courses? In recent months, I watched Peter Galison, Harvard professor of the history of science (and my high school classmate), speak about Harvard's collection of scientific instruments dating back to Benjamin Franklin; Michael Sandel's Harvard Law School ethics class, "Justice"; Duke University's freshman introductory survey class on engineering, Engineering 10; and Stanford design school's 90-minute introductory offering on "how to think like a designer."

Maybe all you want to do is learn a new language or brush up on one studied long ago. Try the free apps for Babble and busuu, which give you spoken vocabulary, phrases and whole conversations to study, repeat and practice.

If all this seems aimless, enter former Paramount president and UC Regent Sherry Lansing's new venture Empowered UCLA Extension (empowered.com), an online, iPad-only learning venture targeted at forty-five to sixty-five-year-olds who want to get certificate-level skills to stay current at their job, be able to get a better job at their current company, or get an entirely new job in such areas as marketing and new media, patient advocacy, health services, financial services, IT and nonprofit management. Tuition is around $13,000 for a one-year program of two courses (if you sign up for the academic year beginning this September, the tuition is approximately $10,000), which includes an iPad loaded with your course materials. Included in the tuition is a career counselor assigned to guide you in your professional development and job search in details large and small, from resume to LinkedIn profile. Lansing has already recruited Hollywood stars such as James Franco, James Gandolfini, George Lopez and Sally Field to promote the site and/or to sponsor scholarships. To give Lansing further credit, this is a well-thought-out, well-designed site and program with an efficient sales force. Within an hour of signing up, I got a phone call; within a week I had spoken to a career counselor. From an organizational and enterprise standpoint, it was impressive.

No one really knows what the lasting impact of all this new online education will be: Will the online democratization of education disrupt and disintermediate the business of education (see what big words you pick up when you study), much like it did the music industry? If a university can charge $100 a course and get 100,000 students, will institutions still need to charge $30,000 to $50,000 a year in tuition? If you can take a Harvard course in your home or even watch it in a classroom in Santa Monica with a local professor and take exams there or at an official testing location, and earn credit at a tenth of the cost, will that lessen the value of a university degree or create a multi-tiered caste system with one type of education for the 1 percent (an Ivy League, on-campus four-year degree) and another for the 99 percent (online or at remote locations, degree or certificate), and will employers care about the distinction? I'll keep you posted on that.

For the young, education may well become another lifelong DIY project; for the majority of their elders, online education affords not only new possibilities but also the joy of discovery, which, as Marcel Proust noted in his study-worthy *In Search of Lost Time,* is the true fountain of youth.

August 8, 2012

ARTIST CHANNA HORWITZ BREAKS THE RULES

Part of the pleasure of seeing a survey show of contemporary art, such as the summer show *Made in LA 2012,* currently at the Hammer Museum, lies in the joy of discovery. There may be artists whose works you recognize, but the WOW! of finding an artist you never knew existed but whose work is fully realized, of-the-moment yet timeless and blows you away, well that is worth the price of admission. And that is what I experienced upon seeing the work of Channa Horwitz.

Imagine my further surprise to discover that Horwitz is, at 80, the oldest artist in the show and that her studio is nearby, in West LA.

At first blush, Horwitz's work featured in *Made in LA 2012* appears to be an intense, even compulsive exploration of a grid taken to the nth degree, forming large-scale patterns that appear both naturalistic (like a diagram of DNA) or man-made (computer switches or circuits) and suggest a mathematical algorithm. The images are both minimalist and conceptual, yet clearly the product of intense craft and artistry. Horwitz, as I learned during a recent visit to her studio, sees her works as exercises in logic, explorations of questions that have arisen out of her past work, as well as her artistic history, and out of the graph paper that she uses.

Horwitz was born in Los Angeles. Her grandfather was Orthodox, although her grandmother did not keep a kosher home. Her parents rebelled against their parents' strictures, embracing the Jazz Age and dancing the Charleston. However by the time they were raising Horwitz, their lives had become conventional: Her father was an appliance repairman, and her mother sold bread.

From an early age, Horwitz wanted to be an artist, something so foreign to her parents, that she said, "they didn't know where I came from. No idea." Life drawing was her passion, and, in 1950, she enrolled in the Art Center, a commercial-art school, that was then located on Third Street (today it is the Art Center College of Design in Pasadena). Horwitz recalled her greatest academic training as being a class on "the structure of a shadow."

"How many people have had a class like that?" she said. However, Horwitz got married and left the school. As she put it, "I left art." For the rest of the decade, she stayed home and raised her three children, until she could afford to purchase oil paint and start painting again.

In 1960, she enrolled in Cal State Northridge's art program, which she described as "a phenomenal experience," largely due to one teacher, artist Connor Everts. Everts was "an exciting man," Horwitz said, not so much as an art teacher, but because he taught her "to climb mountains. Literally." By 1963, she discovered that she "no longer wanted to answer the teacher's problems. I wanted to create my own." When told she could not use two motifs in a single painting, she said, "Why not?"

and went on to create a painting with motifs of deep space and flatness. "I became very excited about pursuing the questions in painting flat." She left the Northridge program.

In 1968, the Los Angeles County Museum of Art invited submissions for a prestigious "Experiments in Art and Technology" program pairing artists with scientists and engineers. Horwitz's application included notations for a proposed sculpture called *Suspension of Vertical Beams.* As Horwitz recalled, "I was suggesting that eight beams be controlled by magnetism; that they would be lightweight beams with a top and cap made of metal, and that they would start out at a base and move to the mid position between the top and the bottom and then each one move according to a plan. But not all at the same time. Each of the eight beams were programmed individually." Her submission was initially accepted for the exhibition, but it was the only piece in the show that was never built. To this day, Horwitz sees it as a lost opportunity for the world of art and for science and technology, as her project prefigured mag-lev trains. "Actually, if they had followed me then and taken me dead seriously, we would have had a bullet train," she said.

That all the other artists in the show were men, caused an outrage. A feminist movement sprouted up around Horwitz; she joined it. This act changed how she felt about other female artists and about being an artist herself. Beforehand, Horwitz freely admitted, "I disliked all women artists." However, getting to know some of her contemporaries, including June Wayne, was, Horwitz said, "so influential in my life. She taught me how to be an artist, a woman artist that's equal to a man. We both have brains. The only thing that the women didn't have was confidence and belief in ourselves."

In 1969, Horwitz divorced her first husband, remarried and moved to a house in Hidden Hills. For much of the next four decades, Horwitz remained hidden there, pursuing her art.

"I retreated," she said. "I had so many questions to ask. And such an incredibly beautiful place to live. What an incredible studio!"

Horwitz said that part of the reason she cut herself off was a "lack of trust in myself." Calling herself a "thief," she said that seeing others' work would be too strong an influence. "I just had to have blinders." The downside was the loneliness.

"With the great freedom to sit on the top of my hill and watch the birds in the thermals it was also lonely. I would create something in the studio and jump for joy, literally jump in the studio and go YIPE! YIPE!" She once got so excited about a finished work that she dragged the female letter carrier in to see it. They became friends.

Not that the art world was totally ignorant of Horwitz; her conceptual pieces were highly regarded, and intermittently her work was included in exhibitions. A little more than five years ago, a gallery owner in Berlin fell in love with Horwitz's work, and he organized exhibitions, visits, talks, leading the art world to reacquaint itself with Horwitz. Michael Solway, who had a gallery in Chinatown, exhibited her here (Solway has since closed his gallery).

For her part, Horwitz said she is less wary of the art world now. "I'm not interested in anything that's happening out there."

When *Pacific Standard Time* was being organized, she was asked to revisit some of her earlier pieces, which she did gladly, feeling that in her old work there was plenty of inspiration for the new. At 80, she said she finds the trip from bed to studio somewhat more treacherous, but once there, her passion for making art is undiminished.

"I'm interested in still pursuing my questions," she said.

Anne Ellegood, Hammer senior curator, first saw Horwitz's work at Solway several years ago. "I was very struck by the work for its incredible detail and beauty coupled with conceptual rigor," Ellegood explained recently. "Channa happened to be there, so we spoke about her work, and I learned that she lives very close to the Hammer. She gave me her number, and soon thereafter I called her and we scheduled a studio visit. I have since been to her studio several times. I encouraged the other curators of *Made in LA* to also visit Channa in her studio, and some of us went together. We then decided unanimously to invite her to be in the biennial."

Horwitz said she was happy to be included in the show, but she is still skeptical about her reception. "No one is going to give me a retrospective," she said. Perhaps the response should be the same as what Horwitz once said to her art professor so many years ago: "Why not?"

August 22, 2012

SEX, SEX, SEX

Arthur Schnitzler's Vienna

One of my favorite New Yorker cartoons features two men in conversation walking down a city street. Surrounding them are dollar signs—in every window, on every car, on everything. The caption reads: "Remember when everything was sex, sex, sex?"

This image came to mind the other afternoon at a dramatic reading by Annabelle Gurwitch and Sam Tsoutsouvas of *Arthur Schnitzler—Being Jewish,* a work based on Schnitzler's own writings as culled by Lorenzo Bellettini, an Austrian scholar. The performance at USC was followed by a panel discussion about Schnitzler and his work, with the speakers including Bellettini, Peter Schnitzler—the documentarian and Schnitzler's grandson—the Austrian journalist Philipp Blom and historian Sharon Gillerman from the Hebrew Union College-Jewish Institute of Religion. The event was moderated by USC historian Paul Lerner (a similar reading and panel had been held earlier in the week at the Getty) and was sponsored by the Max Kade

Institute for Austrian-German-Swiss Studies and the Jerome H. Loucheim School of Judaic Studies at USC.

Schnitzler, who lived from 1862 to 1931, was a playwright, novelist, essayist and diarist who spent most of his life in Vienna. His father, Johann Schnitzler, was a prominent Hungarian-Jewish throat doctor who treated some of Vienna's best-known singers and actors; his mother was the daughter of a physician. Schnitzler also became a throat doctor and continued to practice, even after his writing career took center stage. When he was in his 40s, he married Olga Gussmann, a 21-year-old singer and actress. They had two children, but later separated, in part, according to scholars, because Schnitzler's fame eclipsed hers. They remained friendly for the rest of his life, but separation agreed with Schnitzler; it allowed him to pursue his libertine lifestyle.

Schnitzler is most famous for his play *Reigen* (*Merry-Go-Round*), a series of vignettes of characters amorously linked to one another shown before and after sex, and more popularly known as *La Ronde*, for the film adaptation by Max Ophuls. It is a work that continues to inspire to this day—the most recent version being Fernando Meirelles 2011 film, *360*. Schnitzler's works also inspired Tom Stoppard's *Dalliance*, David Hare's *The Blue Room* and Stanley Kubrick's *Eyes Wide Shut*.

Perhaps no writer since Casanova has paid as much attention to, or has gotten as much literary mileage out of, his numerous sexual encounters. From the age of 17 up until two days before his death, Schnitzler kept a diary—some 8,000 pages, now collected in 10 volumes—that is notable for the casualness with which he describes his sexual encounters, as well as for his obsessiveness; for several years he kept an inventory of each of his orgasms, notated day by day.

In his day, Schnitzler was branded a pornographer and his works were banned, although he was later acclaimed and embraced as one of the most important writers of his era. He was part of a small circle of intellectual lights of fin-de-siècle Vienna that also included his friend Theodor Herzl (although Herzl's Zionism seemed to get on Schnitzler's nerves), and Sigmund Freud, who called Schnitzler his "doppelganger," and who, Freud said, seemed to intuit in his characters the psychological truths Freud had worked so hard to discern. The group also included the essayist Karl Kraus, who was Schnitzler's literary enemy, taking him to task for work Kraus adjudged decadent.

However, after World War I, some dismissed Schnitzler as passé. As the USC panelists made clear, the reasons for his rise and fall were several: He was praised as one of the first writers to use interior monologue and stream of consciousness to define character and attack the established order: In *Anatol,* he described an immature playboy; in *Lieutenant Gustl,* the rigid military code; in *Fräulein Elise,* a young aristocratic Jewish woman's moral dilemma. He was an early master of the short story, and he captured the anomie of a middle and upper class with too much time on its hands. He was critiqued for his amoral characters, for the lack of political engagement in his work, for returning to the same themes over and over again—and he was attacked for being Jewish. Which brings us back to *Schnitzler—Being Jewish.*

The late 19th century in Austria brought forth not only the emancipation of the Jews, but also their rise to the highest levels of Austrian society and culture. It was Jewish families who built the Ringstrasse, filled the opera houses, and in many cases it was Jews who wrote the music, the plays, owned and wrote for the newspapers, magazines and literary journals, crowded the cafes, and who posed for and were patrons of the great artists. Vienna arguably had become the greatest city in the world for the highly successful Jewish population, the majority of whom felt themselves to be completely assimilated and could not imagine a turning back on their bright future ahead.

However, in 1897, Karl Lueger became mayor of Vienna. His Christian Social Party would employ no Jews, and he became among the first in the 20th century to exploit anti-Semitism as a political philosophy. Schnitzler could not have been more surprised. It was Lueger, Schnitzler is supposed to have said, who made Schnitzler realize he was a Jew. It was also Lueger who made the Viennese concerned about politics, a subject the Jewish middle and upper class had become comfortable enough to become disinterested in.

Schnitzler, who was in no way observant, therefore embraced his Jewish identity—he was critical of those, like the poet Hugo von Hofmannsthal, who wanted to deny it, or those like Herzl who felt that fleeing to Palestine was a solution. Jewishness was, for Schnitzler, a consciousness, a racial identity divorced from its spiritual dimension, a quality that he sought to reveal in his characters. Yet, as being Jewish had increasing political consequences, Schnitzler's attitude, like his work, came to appear old-fashioned. Sex had become a luxury. In Vienna, the topic was no longer sex, sex, sex, but politics, politics, politics.

Now, at the 150th anniversary of his birth, Schnitzler seems to be very much in the air—mentioned in the Getty's Klimt exhibition and also making an appearance in LACMA's Kubrick exhibition. When I asked the panel at USC why this was, their answers varied. Peter Schnitzler observed that his grandfather's work comes in and out of style as society itself goes through periods that are more conservative or liberal.

"Art and death, betrayal and [sexual] liaisons are eternal themes," said the journalist Blom, and all of them remain relevant to this day. Yet Schnitzler's work, in which so many characters reach an unhappy end, also contains a warning that regardless of the material comforts and seeming social mobility of the Jews, anti-Semitism never fully goes out of fashion. And that a life without meaning is as eternally alluring, and inevitably unfulfilling, as a merry-go-round of sex, sex, sex.

September 27, 2012

WHAT'S SO GREAT ABOUT STANLEY KUBRICK

On Nov. 1, the Los Angeles County of Museum of Art, (LACMA) in partnership with the Academy of Motion Picture Arts and Sciences (those wonderful folks who bring us the Oscars), will present the first U.S. retrospective of filmmaker Stanley Kubrick, a project developed in partnership with the Kubrick estate, a show that originated at the Deutsches Filmmuseum in Frankfurt, Germany, but will be seen here in a more expanded form.

Kubrick, who died in 1999 at 70, was—for those short of memory or Netflix membership—the Bronx-born filmmaker of such idiosyncratic and varied works as *2001: A Space Odyssey, Dr. Strangelove, A Clockwork Orange, Barry Lyndon, The Shining, Full Metal Jacket* and *Eyes Wide Shut.*

"By featuring this legendary filmmaker and his oeuvre in his first retrospective within the context of an art museum," LACMA director and CEO Michael Govan says in the press materials, "Stanley Kubrick will reevaluate how we define the artist in the 21st century and simultaneously expand LACMA's commitment to exploring the intersection of art and film."

Well: Bravo! Rarely have I read a quote so loaded and so revealing. All you need to know is right there, and all I need do is unpack Govan's quote—which I will do, in reverse order.

To wit: 1. "...expand LACMA's commitment to exploring the intersection of art and film." I take this as a phrase serving two masters: First, it acknowledges that the May Co. building at the corner of Wilshire Boulevard and Fairfax Avenue, which has housed only a smattering of exhibitions and a bunch of LACMA offices, is about to become the home of the new Academy Museum, (although this show will be presented in LACMA's Art of the Americas Building). So museum-wise, it is LACMA that will stand at the intersection of art and film. On a deeper level, as the encyclopedic art museum continues to search for its distinctive place in the local and national museum landscape, it is a canny move to tap into the region's most famous industry, the movie biz. This is hardly the museum's first move in that direction; LACMA exhibitions, such as the recent *Dalí : Painting & Film* and the *Tim Burton* show were also ventures into the intersections of high and popular art.

Which brings us to...

2. "Stanley Kubrick will reevaluate how we define the artist in the 21st century." Museums, although most often slower moving than the rest of society, are being forced to rethink what they do, how they do it and who they do it for. So, for example, the Annenberg Space for Photography exhibits at its centerpiece digitally projected images—it is a gallery that is not really about what is on the walls, so much as what can capture the attention and imaginations, camera-roll style, of an Instagram-saturated generation. The Annenberg Space, like the downtown-LA Grammy Museum, which juxtaposes cultural artifacts and au-

diovisuals in curated shows, have been successful at breaking ground with regard to what a museum can do.

By contrast, Los Angeles' veteran Museum of Contemporary Art (MOCA), under the directorship of Jeffrey Deitch, has, in its attempt to redefine art as fashion and to outsource its curatorial function, been roundly criticized (and deservedly so) for abandoning its mission and its legacy as the place for visionary, large-scale art historical shows that force us to think— and rethink— the work of contemporary artists such as Robert Rauschenberg and Arshile Gorky, among others.

Finally, 3. "By featuring this legendary filmmaker and his oeuvre..." You know any time the word French word "oeuvre" (body of work) is used, that the other French term "auteur" (literally, author) is not far behind. And if Kubrick is a "legendary filmmaker," what exactly is his legend?

Glad you asked: Legend has it that Kubrick, a poor student, became absorbed by photography as a teenager, selling his first photo to Look magazine at the age of 16 and eventually becoming a staff photographer there. One of his friends from high school, Alex Singer, was working in the offices of the newsreel *March of Time,* and he helped Kubrick get his first directing assignment, *Day of the Fight,* about a boxer. Kubrick shot, edited and did almost all the work on the film, thereby garnering firsthand a wide education on every facet of filmmaking.

Kubrick's Hollywood career took off with a pair of Kirk Douglas dramas, *Paths of Glory* and *Spartacus,* which he followed with two satirical works starring Peter Sellers, *Lolita* and *Dr. Strangelove.* In those early four films, the actors were the stars. By contrast, though his *A Clockwork Orange* made Malcolm McDowell a star, it was Kubrick who got top billing for the film.

With the release of *2001: A Space Odyssey* in 1968, Kubrick's use of music, his attention to technical details, and the ambition and talent of what went on the screen made the announcement loud and clear (and at great length) that Kubrick had become his films' star. From then on, (with the possible exception of Jack Nicholson in *The Shining* in 1980), audiences went to see a Kubrick film, not to see who was in it.

The exhibition at LACMA promises to reveal the influences and references Kubrick found as inspiration, as well as what archival material, photographs, props, costumes and annotated scripts he used for his technical and artistic innovations.

In his later years, Kubrick became obsessed with controlling every aspect of production, and his research leading up to a project—his perfectionism and his inventive use of special effects, lighting and camera movement—would impact the work of a generation of filmmakers to follow and would add to the cult-like reverence for his work. It would also contribute to the eventual stagnation of his career—he rarely left England and almost as rarely left his home. He spent years on projects that he later abandoned. The result was his work suffered, as evidenced by the fiasco that was his final film, the Arthur Schnitzler-inspired, Tom Cruise-Nicole Kidman vehicle, *Eyes Wide Shut*.

Film aficionados see Kubrick as a genius. But he was also a Jewish boy from the Bronx who became sealed away from the world by a lens, controlling his narratives on an editing table. Neither he nor his parents were in any way Jewishly observant, but Kubrick, in England, loved to surround himself with Jewish friends, screenwriters and colleagues. His acknowledged great influence as a director was Max Ophuls, whose camera movements he adopted (Ophuls, in turn, gave credit for his use of reverse-dolly shots to director Anatole Litvak—all Jewish directors).

Late in life, Kubrick spent years on a Holocaust-inspired project called *Aryan Papers* (which I had heard was based, in part, on Louis Begley's *Wartime Lies*), immersing himself in research on the Shoah. There are many apocryphal accounts of why he abandoned this undertaking, but perhaps it was just that the film would have required Kubrick to go to a place that he could not, or would not.

The Kubrick retrospective at LACMA will, no doubt, give each of us much to consider, not only in terms of a career and legacy, but also in helping us to examine whether the ephemera of Kubrick's life's work can tell us what's truly great about Stanley Kubrick.

September 11, 2012

RITA ROCKS HER PERSIAN ROOTS

On Nov. 1, Israel's most popular and enduring pop icon, Rita Yahan-Farouz, known the world over simply as Rita, will appear at UCLA's Royce Hall, along with a special band assembled for this tour. She will perform songs from throughout her career, in Hebrew, as well as songs from *My Joys* (HaSmachot Shelanu), her most recent hit album, which includes lyrics in Farsi performed with Middle Eastern flavor and gypsy rhythms that have become surprise dance hits in Israel, as well as in Iran where, although not permitted, her songs have found underground success—achieving a musical bridge between two peoples that is a peaceful counterpoint to their countries' respective leaders beating drums of war. In advance of her Los Angeles date, Rita spoke by phone from Israel about her life, career and the concert she will perform in LA The following is an edited version of that conversation.

Tom Teicholz: What brought your parents to Israel in 1970, at a time when life for Iranian Jews under the shah was relatively good?

Rita Yahan-Farouz: Actually, at that time we lived in Tehran in the same neighborhood as many of the Iranian army's generals. Our parents told us not to tell anyone there that we were Jews.

TT: So you experienced discrimination then?

Rita: It was not so bad, but that was something they told us when we were little. We went to a Muslim school, and every morning they would say the Muslim prayers in class. One day, the teacher asked my sister, who was 14, to do the Muslim prayers, and she said she can't do that. She was so embarrassed. When she came back home, she said that all the other girls in the class had looked at her like she fell out of the sky, because she didn't know the prayers. She was crying. When my father came home after work at night, he asked what happened, and she told him. And he said, "Well, I think this is a good time to leave to Israel."

TT: Growing up in Israel, did your family cling to Iranian traditions or culture? Were you raised speaking Farsi?

Rita: We didn't do anything really. Not on purpose. My mother had a great voice, and she used to sing Persian songs all the time at home when she was cooking, when she was working or when we had dinners with guests; after dinner she would sing for us. We didn't study Persian. Exactly as much Persian as I knew when I left Iran when I was 8 years old is all the Persian I know. Maybe after working on this record, my Persian is better than it was before, but I can't really speak or understand Persian as well as my father or mother.

TT: What were the circumstances that brought about the album *My Joys*?

Rita: I was in the middle of recording another album [in Hebrew]. Then I started to work with a band that is Moroccan and rock and roll, and I had a show with them [The Mind Church/ Knesiyat Hasekhel]...And I suddenly felt something—I don't know how to explain it—but I knew that I had to stop the record I was making, and I had no doubt that I must do something completely different. I thought that I was going to do a world music record—something like taking songs from around the Middle East. But every time I went to look for something, I went to the box of records, the singles that my mother brought from Iran. Each one of those singles, I would say, "This is a great song." Suddenly, after two, three months of working, I understood that all the songs that I chose are Persian, and each song means something to me; that I grew up on those songs. This is the soundtrack of my life, of my childhood, of my family.

TT: Even if these are the songs of your childhood, the way you sing them, and the music that surrounds the lyrics, is a wholly contemporary world-music interpretation.

Rita: I'm not a classic Persian singer. I studied classical music, but I sing pop and rock, and I've been out of Iran for so many years [that] this is a fusion of all that I am. I was lucky; all the musicians that I played with [on *My Joys*] are really artists who are geniuses with their instruments and often are touring abroad. My dream was to take this [sound] to the stage. Sometimes you can't really translate it to the stage, but everyone who I dreamt of is with me. What is happening with all these musicians in the show is that we are like a gypsy band that is going from country to country, state to state. This experience is like a world of different colors—or like the aroma or scent of something completely different—what people say is that the show lifts them up to a place of happiness; that you go back home much happier. I am very, very lucky to be there [with the audience] for this moment of celebration, of life.

TT: This album has become a success in Israel and also an underground success Iran. That must be very gratifying.

Rita: It's amazing, you know. I get so many amazing e-mails from all over the world, from Iranians in Iran who say, "Thank you for showing our real culture to the world," because nowadays we are only talking about bombs and dark, dark, things.

TT: It's somewhat ironic that your musical career began in the Israeli army and now you are waging heavy peace.

Rita: (laughs) But even in my army [service] I was singing. This is the only weapon I know and the only real working weapon in the world. Music is responsible for so many changes and revolutions in the world.

TT: You have performed several times for Prime Minister Netanyahu. Has he spoken to you about your new songs?

Rita: No. We have not spoken of that.

TT: And would you perform in Iran if invited?

Rita: Of course! I would be so glad to do that! I will be thrilled to do that. And that time will arrive soon, I believe.

TT: Tell me about what we can expect of your LA concert.

Rita: Most of the concerts were for Israelis. This time the songs are from my entire repertoire in Hebrew, and those Persian songs fit in amazingly well together. I think it will be something really new for me and for my audience.

TT: LA has a large Iranian community and a very prominent Iranian-Jewish community. What are you hoping to share with them?

Rita: Happiness, joy and amazing, amazing music and celebration.

October 24, 2012

LARRY MILLER'S BED OF ROSES

In person, Larry Miller, president of Sit 'n Sleep, is less "Crazy Eddie" (fast-talking, exuberant salesman) and more "Uncle Larry" (the gregarious, warmhearted, favorite family relative). When I went to visit him in his executive offices in Gardena, next to his 240,000-square-foot warehouse, he struck me, no kidding, as a man who sleeps well at night.

Larry Miller is proud, and justifiably so, of all that he has accomplished and all that is right in his world. His 28 stores in Southern California (and counting) sell more mattresses per store, according to their Web site, than any other retailer in the country. His son Andrew ("Drew") is coming into the business, starting on the advertising and marketing side. His daughter Danielle is going to be a doctor and is currently the project manager for a successful charity, Cell-Ed. He gets along well with his ex-wife, is happily remarried and recently went on the first real vacation of his life since he started his business.

Miller, along with his business partners and employees, is very charitable: He is a large donor to and honoree of Jewish Vocational Service (JVS), a nondenominational nonprofit that helps people find new careers and employment, and the Scott Newman Foundation, whose focus is drug education. Sit 'n

Sleep has also partnered with Habitat for Humanity to provide families with new beds; his employees organized a charity golf tournament and, in general, where possible, as Miller recently said, "I try not to say no."

However, that was not always the case. As Miller recounted, more than 25 years ago, on the very day his daughter was about to be born, he found himself in trying circumstances.

Miller said he always had an interest in business. He was working even before he became a teenager, be it a paper route or selling something. However, after graduating from California State University, Northridge, he decided that he was through taking orders.

"My big sister told me what to do, my parents told me what to do, my principals at school told me what to do," Miller said.

He didn't like bosses who motivated through fear or who were mean. So instead, he went to work with his father, Phil, but that posed challenges of its own. At first, his father was tough. "He didn't want to give up control," Miller said.

They started a franchise business in Culver City that sold convertible sofas—which, Miller recalled, "just didn't work." They ended the franchise and kept the single store, naming it Sit 'n Sleep. Miller and his father began the business with $10,000 each—and they were soon stretched thin.

During a trip to Japan in the early 1970s, Miller had discovered the futon—an inexpensive cotton mattress that could be used for bedding or folded as a couch. He felt that the time was right to offer them in the United States and persuaded his father to carry them: thus Sit 'n Sleep. And they sold, bringing in a younger demographic of students, teenagers and first-time buyers, which bought the business some breathing room. That small success accomplished something else: It helped Miller earn the respect of his father, who would now trust Miller in the direction of the business.

However, they still weren't making enough for Miller to live on. Often people would walk into the store and solicit them for a charitable donation. Miller had to say no.

"They thought because we had a business we could afford to be charitable," he said.

The futons, Miller said, were only "a short-term fix." To succeed, Miller realized, he would have to sell branded merchandise, such as mattresses, which he began to carry.

One day a salesman from a mattress manufacturer came to visit the store. He had to walk past all the futons to get to the mattresses stacked against the back wall.

"Maybe you should consider moving them further up front," the salesman suggested. "So maybe you'd sell more of them."

That was when Miller realized that he was in the mattress business. However, things would get worse before they got better.

The day his daughter was to be born, his business was $175,000 in debt; his personal credit card debt was $130,000. He owed the government money for taxes he couldn't pay. He needed $10,000 to pay for mattresses, and he knew the check wouldn't clear. It was a Friday, and he gave the mattress supplier the check, knowing that he would have to make it good by Monday. He left for the hospital hoping his partner, Nelson Bercier (who is also his brother-in-law), would make enough in sales to help them cover the check. Soon after, his daughter was born.

"The greatest gift I ever got," Miller said.

After he left the hospital, he called his partner: "What did we do?" Bercier told him there were no sales. Miller went home, and although he wasn't a drinker he opened a bottle of scotch. "What have I done?" he asked himself.

Monday the bank called, asking him about a $10,000 check. Miller promised he would bring the funds to cover the check by noon. From his credit cards he cobbled together $9,000. In the office lock box there was a $600 check. The bank manager asked him again whether there would be enough money to clear his $10,000 check. Miller promised there would be—he just didn't know how. He explained that he was leaving to pick up his wife and new daughter from the hospital. The manager agreed to clear the check anyhow.

Miller then made a promise to himself. "If I ever became successful, I would give back," and that if he could, he would try not to say no.

How did he turn things around? First, he decided to run the business based on what mattered to him and what he thought would matter to the customer: selection, the largest selection of mattresses available; a knowledgeable sales staff who are all, in Miller's words, "mensches" (regardless of gender, race, color or creed); and price, which he is able to offer based on the volume of mattresses he sells.

Let me say this: Miller is a compelling salesman. As he put it to me, "Listen, you are born in a mattress, you die in a mattress. You make love; you give birth. You have romance; you have tears. You dream; you eat. You're on your computer; you're entertained. You spend more time there than anywhere else." Or in another words: "What's more important to your health than a good night's sleep?"

What turned around Miller's business, however, was advertising. At first, he advertised in the *Herald Examiner*, then in the *LA Weekly*. KABC talk radio offered to give him credit to run late-night radio ads. At first an announcer read the ads, but Miller's father thought they were terrible, and Miller complained.

"He said, 'Listen, smartass, why don't you come in and do it yourself?' "

At first, Miller said, "I was scared to death." By his own admission, he was terrible. However, LA sportscaster Stu Nahan was in the studio and he coached Miller.

Sit 'n Sleep advertised on more radio shows, and in 1991 Miller got a call that Howard Stern's show was coming to the LA market. Miller had never heard of Stern, but Sit 'n Sleep put its ads on his show. "They were hugely successful. Our business went from $1 million to $2 million in sales. It was a big deal. In 1993, we went on TV, our business went up fifty percent more. Then we built up the Culver City store to the highest-grossing mattress store in the country, which it still is. And since then we opened twenty-seven more stores."

More sales meant more bargaining power with the mattress manufacturers, being able to hire and pay better salespeople and continue to deliver on selection, superior sales staff and price.

When the recession hit, Miller decided he needed to give the customer a better reason to buy a new mattress. At the same time, he visited his elderly mother and noticed that she was sleeping on a lumpy mattress. He offered to get her a new one. I haven't had this one that long, she said. He looked at the mattress tag and discovered it was sixteen years old. He did more research and discovered that a mattress doubles in weight over eight years, filled with dust mites, dead skin and other unmentionables. So he started a "replace every eight years" campaign, which Miller is quick to point out has been good for the entire industry, not just Sit 'n Sleep.

Over the past decades, many mattress companies have gone out of business and new mattress stores seem to pop up on corner after corner. Yet Sit 'n Sleep continues to grow.

"I try to take good care of the customers, like they are family. I do. I care," Miller said, reiterating that Sit 'n Sleep gives them "the best selection, the best knowledge, gives them technology—nobody else has—a body diagnostic computer that we have exclusively for Southern California...nobody does the business we do. I try to get deals that my customers will be thrilled with."

Did I want to scream, "You're killing me, Larry"? I did not. I was reminded about the story of Lyndon Johnson, who took the podium after receiving a lavish description of his attributes and accomplishments. "Thank you for that introduction," Johnson supposedly said, "I only wish my parents were here to hear it: My father would have enjoyed what you have so generously said of me—and my mother would have believed it."

To spend time with Miller is to believe him when he says, "I actually think I'm doing people a favor—I believe that and I'm proud of what we do. I'm a lucky guy. I never in my life thought that I'd have what I have or be able to do what I've done. I'm a lucky man."

October 26, 2012

WAS LINCOLN THE FIRST JEWISH PRESIDENT?

Abraham Lincoln has been dead for almost 150 years, yet suddenly he's everywhere. At the Skirball Cultural Center, you can see an original copy of the Emancipation Proclamation, signed by Lincoln, amid an impressive array of founding American documents. The Huntington Library is host to two stunning and deeply engrossing Civil War exhibitions, *A Just Cause: Voices of the Civil War* and *A Strange and Fearful Interest: Death, Mourning, and Memory in the American Civil War.* And on screens everywhere, there's Steven Spielberg's *Lincoln.*

After visiting the exhibitions, watching *Lincoln* was almost surreal—photographs I had just seen and documents I had just read came to life. Daniel Day-Lewis, for his part, seemed to embody Lincoln so completely at certain moments, it was as if he, too, were convinced he actually was Lincoln. At the same time, Spielberg's Lincoln is portrayed in more personal and intimate terms than ever before on film: shown speaking to soldiers, to the war wounded, to family members and advisers; shown being both compassionate and passionate in his advocacy; and seeming something of a sly fox—always with a story, anecdote or joke at the ready to liven a room, make a point or close a deal.

After seeing the movie, I got to thinking about whether this Hollywood studio film, which was written and directed by Jewish-Americans (Tony Kushner and Spielberg, respectively), and which depicts the quintessential American as portrayed by Day-Lewis (whose mother is Jewish), is, in fact, a Jewish version of history in and of itself, a throwback to the days when Hollywood's moguls, themselves Jewish-Americans, made movies about a seemingly non-Jewish America through the filter of their own very Jewish perspective.

Which raises the question: Has Spielberg given us a Jewish Lincoln? Or is it that Lincoln was "Jewish" in his temperament, values and actions: consumed by social justice in his fighting a war to abolish slavery; Moses-like in leading a people to freedom; talmudic in his use of disputation among a "team of rivals" to lead the nation; alternately morose and jovial (who doesn't know that type?)? Add to all this that he died during Passover.

Set during the first four months of 1865, and centered on January, the month during which Lincoln lobbied the House of Representatives to pass the 13th Amendment, the film depicts a Lincoln more human, more flawed than we have ever seen on screen. Spielberg and Kushner contrive to show where Lincoln may have overstepped his authority, suspending habeas corpus and acting by executive fiat, yet the president is allowed to argue in his own defense the legality of his actions. This Lincoln is driven to incorporate the prohibition of slavery into the Constitution because he knows the legal importance of that document and because he fears what will follow if he doesn't accomplish this before the war ends. We also see Lincoln's failings—as a father, husband and friend, as well as in his anger when it flares.

Compassion, charity and the pursuit of justice—these values, which we identify as Jewish values—are what inform the Spielberg-Kushner Lincoln: This is a president who seeks freedom for the slaves, who wants to heal the nation, is devoted to his young son, who visits the sick and mourns the dead. Sound familiar? While they might also be described as American values, even Christian values, it is understood that Spielberg and Kushner know them as the Jewish values of tikkun olam (repairing the world), tzedakah (charitable giving), bikur holim (visiting the sick) and gemilut hasadim (acts of lovingkindness).

"Joint Resolution Submitting 13th Amendment to the States, signed by Abraham Lincoln and Congress." Abraham Lincoln Papers, Manuscript Division, Library of Congress.

There is one more way that this "Lincoln" conforms to an "Old Hollywood" tradition of Jews using the movies to redefine American history: The film contains no mention of Jews or Judaism.

It is historical fact, however, that Lincoln was very much a friend of the Jews, and he was much loved by the Jewish community, both in his day and after his death. There is even some reason to believe that Lincoln himself had Jewish forebears.

In Illinois, Abraham Jonas, the first Jewish settler west of the Allegheny Mountains, served in the Illinois legislature with Lincoln and was, in Lincoln's words, his "most valued friend." Louis Dembitz Brandeis, a Jew from Kentucky, was a Lincoln delegate to the 1860 Republican Convention and was reportedly the first to vote to nominate Lincoln for president. As president, Lincoln appointed the first Jew to serve as a foreign consul. More important, Lincoln was the first and only president to revoke an official U.S. act of anti-Semitism, canceling Gen. Ulysses S. Grant's order barring Jewish peddlers from selling to

Union troops. In Washington, one of Lincoln's best friends was Isachar Zacharie, a Jewish doctor from England who treated him and became his friend. His photographer, Samuel Alschuler, was Jewish. And, according to the Rosewater Family papers donated to the American Jewish Archives, Edward Rosewater, while serving as a telegrapher in the War Department in Washington, D.C., during the Civil War, came to know Lincoln, who would often come to Rosewater to dictate and receive communications. It was Rosewater who dispatched the Emancipation Proclamation to the world.

Even more intriguing was the claim that Rabbi Isaac M. Wise, author of the Union Prayer Book and founder of Hebrew Union College, delivered in his funeral address for Lincoln in Cincinnati in 1865: "Brethren, the lamented Abraham Lincoln believed himself to be bone from our bone and flesh from our flesh. He supposed himself to be a descendant of Hebrew parentage. He said so in my presence. And, indeed, he preserved numerous features of the Hebrew race, both in countenance and character."

Lincoln, really Jewish? There are some tantalizing clues. He was named Abraham, for his grandfather, Abraham, who died when Lincoln's own father was quite young; his paternal great-great-grandfather was named Mordecai, as was his uncle. Their last name derives from the city from which they emigrated, Lincoln in England (many Jews adopted as family names the city they hailed from). The city of Lincoln, it is interesting to note, is famous for being home to one of England's oldest and most important Jewish communities, as well as for saving its Jews during the 12th century Crusader riots. However, Abraham Lincoln's son Robert denied that his family was of Jewish ancestry, saying that his father was merely jesting when he spoke with Rabbi Wise.

Still, it is not so hard to believe that Lincoln, who never professed a faith other than citing the Ten Commandments in Exodus, saw himself as a descendant of Jewish tradition, for where did his sense of justice and fairness come from if not from Mosaic law, or his belief that a mere amendment to the Constitution would do more than an army to win a war?

Although some historians have suggested that Lincoln suffered from depression, in Spielberg's rendering he is not so much depressed as hobbled by the weight of the war, the war dead and the wounded veterans he has met; his wife (in a powerful performance by Sally Field), besotted by grief for a dead son and fearful of losing another to the war, both prods him and adds to his burden. All these factors contribute to Lincoln's urgency to end slavery by passing the 13th Amendment before the war ends with the South. To do so, Lincoln uses every arrow in his quiver—cajoling, strong arming and making personal appeals to get the votes he needs. We see politics in action and understand that great change comes from great will—knowing when not to compromise—and always at some cost.

In press notes for the film, Kushner describes Spielberg and his decision to narrow the focus of the film to the passage of the 13th Amendment: "We both felt it was incredibly timely, because in this day and age when so many people have lost faith in the idea of governance it's a story that shows you can achieve miraculous, beautiful things through the democratic system. That month was also a lens though which you could see Lincoln with real clarity. It had all the ingredients that characterize him—his family life, his emotional life and his political genius."

Spielberg, who very much wanted to show both the leader and the man, describes Lincoln as someone "who was continually looking inside himself."

The Lincoln of Spielberg's film is very much in evidence in both the Skirball and Huntington exhibitions—which together include more important US historical artifacts and documents on display than anywhere in the world outside Washington, DC, and more than have ever been seen here before. The exhibitions include rough drafts and original copies of the Declaration of Independence, the Constitution, the Bill of Rights, the Emancipation Proclamation and the 13th Amendment (ending slavery), as well as one of the largest displays of Mathew Brady and Alexander Gardner's haunting photos of the Civil War dead, and original materials relating to the end of the Civil War, the assassination of Lincoln and his funeral procession.

Creating the United States, at the Skirball through Feb. 17, illustrates the process by which the U.S. became a functioning democracy. We are treated to original publications by Benjamin Franklin from as early as 1750, suggesting a confederation of states; engravings by Paul Revere (yes, the silversmith midnight rider); and original correspondence by John Hancock, George Washington and Thomas Jefferson (along with a facsimile of Jefferson's signing desk). There before your eyes are the Stamp Tax, a tea box, an engraving depicting the Boston Tea Party and Jefferson's rough draft of the Declaration of Independence.

A second section documents how the Constitution came into being, even how its iconic preamble, "We the people of the United States, in order to form a more perfect Union," was composed; a third section is devoted to the Bill of Rights; and a final fourth section highlights how the political conversation begun in these documents continues throughout the history of this country. It is humbling to stand before an original copy of the Emancipation Proclamation, signed by Lincoln, as well as a copy of the 13th Amendment and the 19th Amendment, granting women the right to vote.

Reading these documents, it becomes "self-evident" that the argument over slavery began before there even was a United States (Franklin urged that the Republic not countenance the practice). And yet, slavery remained unresolved until Lincoln issued the Emancipation Proclamation in 1863, followed by the ratification of the 13th Amendment in 1865. Lincoln is shown as just part of a long line of leaders who fostered, interpreted and extended the meaning of that singular phrase, "all men are created equal."

At the Huntington, the focus is more specifically on the Civil War, with two exhibits featuring rare documents and photographs from the library's collection: *A Just Cause: Voices of the Civil War,* which runs through Jan. 7, and *A Strange and Fearful Interest: Death, Mourning, and Memory in the American Civil War,* which will close Jan. 14.

A Just Cause, whose title is drawn from a letter Lincoln wrote to Gen. Ulysses S. Grant, includes letters, diaries and other writings by Lincoln, Jefferson Davis and Frederick Douglass, as well as from Union and Confederate soldiers and their families. The Civil War was, one veteran said, "a battle of ideas punctuated by artillery." The exhibition demonstrates the complexity of a conflict in which each side felt it was fighting with God on its side. The South felt that States should have the right to secede; to them the issue was not slavery but abolition. The North tried just as hard to say that slavery was not the issue, it was the South attempting to secede and their rebellion that they were fighting. Yet it was slavery that stood at the center of the rift, not just its morality, legality or its role in the economy of the South, but also whether a nation could be half-free and half-not. The Civil War was so devastating that after the first years, many people were no longer sure what they were fighting for—their states, their livelihoods, their way of life or the abolition of slavery. Passage of the 13th Amendment by Congress on Jan. 31, 1865, heralded the surrender of the Confederate troops a few months after.

A Strange and Fearful Interest includes rare photographs of the Civil War and, most hauntingly, of Civil War dead. Image after image shows slain soldiers abandoned like deadwood on the battleground. When these images were first shown in New York during the war, they drew huge crowds—and provoked editorials about how distanced the general population was becoming from the war.

Although Lincoln is not present in most of the images, his presence remains at the center of it all. To some, in both the North and South, he was seen as a tyrant, abusing executive privilege, bypassing Congress by issuing the Emancipation Proclamation, violating the law, obsessed with ending slavery at any cost, including the deaths of tens of thousands of soldiers; in the South, the problem was not slavery, but abolition. To others, however, Lincoln was a great man, the moral force, the father of the nation.

Also among the Huntington's artifacts are engravings that speak to the assassination of Lincoln, including a rare handbill offering a reward for information leading to the capture of the conspirators in his assassination, as well as photos of their hanging and pictures of the grieving crowds watching Lincoln's funeral procession, from Washington, DC, to Springfield, Ill. These images offer a deep sense of Lincoln's canonization and show how a figure so controversial in life became revered in death.

Taken together, the Lincoln that emerges from the film and these exhibitions is well read, deeply versed in the Old Testament, self-taught, someone who has both a deep belief in the legal system and the rule of law, so much so that he understands that a nation is made more robust by challenges and emendations to those laws. Lincoln tended to be a loner, prone to solitary contemplation, who nevertheless maintained deep friendships, was curious about people from all walks of life as well as all political bents and all races, and could be as gregarious as he was at times taciturn. He loved jokes and off-color stories and told them with great relish. He was, in all respects, a mensch.

No one should miss the chance of seeing, in tandem, these rare documents and photos telling our history, and the film, depicting a Lincoln who, if not our co-religionist, was most certainly a man with whom we share a common heritage.

For evidence, you need look no further than the prayerful words with which Lincoln concluded his second inaugural address on March 4, 1865, just weeks after the passage of the 13th Amendment, days before the end of the Civil War and a mere few weeks before his own death:

"With malice toward none, with charity for all, with firmness in the right as God gives us to see the right, let us strive on to finish the work we are in, to bind up the nation's wounds, to care for him who shall have borne the battle and for his widow and his orphan, to do all which may achieve and cherish a just and lasting peace among ourselves and with all nations."

November 14, 2012

SEE THE FAR AWAY BEFORE IT GOES AWAY

Last spring, I visited the National Museum of Anthropology in Mexico City and then, a month later, traveled to Chichen Itza, the 1,000-plus-year-old Mayan ruin. Both times I was struck by, on the one hand, the scientific, mathematical and engineering sophistication of the ancient Mayan culture and, on the other, the thought of the powerful hallucinogens they must have imbibed for them to come up with their phantasmagoric visions of the afterlife—let alone their brutal ceremonies. (Just one example: a rugbylike game where the penalty was to have your head chopped off to be used as a ball.)

I mention this because even when we visit sites of early civilization—Athens, Rome, Jerusalem, Angkor Wat, Pompeii, Machu Picchu or Petra—ancient wisdom seems like ancient history, evidence of a culture that no longer exists. It is very easy to believe that we have evolved, that modern society has progressed. But the real loss remains elusive: What might we have learned from these extinct peoples?

No Strangers: Ancient Wisdom in a Modern World, at the Annenberg Space for Photography, transports us through photographs to places most of us will never see, far-away corners of the earth where indigenous people still practice their traditional cultures. Curated by anthropologist Wade Davis, whose book-turned-film, *The Serpent and the Rainbow,* explored Haitian voodoo culture and sought to explain zombies by studying psychotropic substances, *No Strangers* features work by 24 photographers, as well as a short documentary about the photographers' work. The exhibition is organized around several themes, including: The Circle of Life, Our Shared Origins, Ancient Wisdom, Sacred Geography, Endangered, Globalization, Ritual and Passages, Beauty, Quest for Spirit and Joy of Culture.

Think you've seen everything? How about Mongolian women herding reindeer? Or an Inuit hunter striding an ice floe off Baffin Island in Nunavut, Canada? They're here, along with a group of Shaolin monks from China's Henan Province shown hanging from their toes, male charm dancers at the annual Gerewol festival in Niger and the courtship ritual practiced in the central highlands of Papua New Guinea.

The images capture the last nomads in the rainforests of Borneo, Tibetan Buddhists in Nepal, the ceremonies of the Lakota tribe in South Dakota, an Ethiopian bull-jumping ceremony and the bonding of mother and child in countries all over the world.

The exhibition also poses a fundamental question, according to the press materials: "What does it mean to be human and alive?"

The show considers how we experience the world in such diverse ways, and how, despite such extreme differences, a shared humanity still exists. It also explores what such surviving ancient customs and tribal beliefs might offer our modern society not only because they are valuable historically, but also because they're disappearing fast. As our world encroaches on theirs, as rainforests and glaciers shrink, and climate changes, these cultures will be forced to adapt—and many will vanish. And if the world one day becomes a globalized, homogenized culture—what else will be lost?

Davis, a National Geographic explorer-in-residence, is also an ethno-botanist. For more than 30 years, he has studied plants in the Amazon and Andes, living among native tribes, as well as traveling all over the globe. Davis is also a passionate spokesperson for diversity—in plants, in culture and for the planet. This exhibition is an expression of that sensibility, celebrating the fact that life, for all beings, is a journey from birth to death, however different the path.

It is also a reminder that there is a price to pay when civilizations are reduced to memento mori, when a people's rituals and way of life fade away—when what is becomes what was.

November 20, 2012

THE WINDING ROAD TO *OTHER DESERT CITIES*

In Hollywood, the logline for this story would be: A playwright who has outwitted his demons to find balance in his life, has, after a devastating TV experience, returned to the stage with a play whose plot twist is as transformative to its actors, and to the audience's assumptions about the characters, as writing it was for the playwright. The play is a success off-Broadway and then a bigger success on Broadway. And then, as validation and final vindication, he brings it to Los Angeles.

The thing is, this is not fiction, it is true.

The playwright: Jon Robin Baitz.

The play: *Other Desert Cities,* which opens at the Mark Taper Forum on Nov. 28.

The TV show on whose ruins the play was built: *Brothers & Sisters.*

But the story, like the play itself, is so much better, and deeper, in its details.

Like Baitz's early work, *The Substance of Fire,* in which a historical inflection point (the Holocaust) tears at the fabric of a family, in *Other Desert Cities,* a family's longstanding conflicts over the Vietnam War and its aftermath threaten to rip them asunder. *Other Desert Cities* is set during a dysfunctional family reunion in Palm Springs at Christmas. The participants include a prominent patrician politician as paterfamilias; his steely, assimilated matriarch wife; the matriarch's sister, whose embrace of her Jewish ethnicity stands in stark contrast to the matriarch; and their grown children—a son who works in reality TV; and his sister, the prodigal daughter, a novelist about to publish a memoir laying bare the family secrets.

It turns out, as I remarked to Baitz when we met recently for lunch in Culver City, that every character in the play is living a lie—just not the one they thought they were living. It is this layering of the personal and political with questions of identity and obligation—and a yearning to, in E.M. Forster's dictum, "only connect"—that distinguishes and elevates Baitz's work.

A native of Los Angeles, Baitz spent most of his childhood and teenage years abroad. His father, Edward, was an executive for the Carnation Co., posted to Brazil and then South Africa. Living in Brazil under a military dictatorship, and in South Africa during apartheid, sensitized Baitz to the way politics can convulse both society and family."I knew very early that whatever this norm was, it couldn't hold," he said of South Africa. "At a certain point, I simply became afraid that it would turn into a cataclysm."

At the same time, given Baitz's father's position as an American businessman working in countries with great domestic disturbances, and the characterization of the father in *Other Desert Cities* as the keeper of secrets, I wondered whether Baitz's father had worked for the CIA. It turns out that Baitz's father had, as a young man, worked for the National Security Agency, and although Baitz does not know whether his father remained involved, he says, "I felt there was a lot going on that I was not privy to, that there was an interesting subtextual awareness and political savvy." His father, Baitz said, "had a certain expertise in how people work all over the Third World." He tangled with the Afrikaner government, and Baitz recalls his father, later in life, "being debriefed by someone from the noncovert section of the CIA."

Although the future writer returned to the United States in time to graduate from Beverly Hills High School, he has remained "slightly an outsider," keenly attuned to political disturbance. "I live in a state where I am aware that, whatever the social contract is, it's quite fragile—here, too. The play comes out of that," he said.

"As we reach a point where a dialogue is no longer possible in terms of the left and the right in this country, the play actually tries to address that gridlock," he added.

Baitz's writing is not moralistic, nor does he seek to badger us into his political point of view. Rather, he is searching for a greater emotional truth.

Both *Brothers & Sisters* and *Other Desert Cities* describe a family that in no way reads Jewish, with the exception of Uncle Saul (played by Ron Rifkin) in the former, and Aunt Silda (Judith Light on Broadway; Jeannie Berlin in Los Angeles) in the latter. I recalled to him, with pleasure, that moment in *Brothers & Sisters* when it finally dawned on me that Sally Fields' character must be Jewish, and how strange their Chanukah-Christmas was, with Saul intoning Hebrew words that indeed seemed foreign to the rest of the family.

That was not the case in his own family, Baitz explained. "My family was deeply traditional. On my father's side, they started a fund for the Jewish Home for the Aged in Washington, DC, for which they sponsored concerts; my grandmother sang Yiddish songs, performed. I went to temple, I went to a Jewish school; I laid tefillin—everything."

The WASP-y Jew he writes about is autobiographical insofar as it reflects Baitz's own Anglophilia. "I'm always slightly removed," he said, explaining that he's no longer observant because "I can't surrender my curiosity over to an orthodoxy of any sort.... To me, my iteration of Jewishness is simply 'Do Unto Others'—that is the cornerstone for me, the be-all and end-all, and I don't even think that even depends on an Old Testament God."

I mentioned to him that *Other Desert Cities* brings to mind Philip Roth's *American Pastorale,* which is also a story of American Jews at the apotheosis of assimilation brought low by their daughter's radical antiwar action. However, Roth's vision in *Pastorale* is profoundly pessimistic, while Baitz's is far more hopeful. Baitz acknowledged the similarities, but said, "I think my experience and Roth's are very different. I can't afford the level of skepticism, whether sexual skepticism or cultural skepticism. I can't afford to...I'm much more outward-directed...I think I am slightly sentimental about what is great in this country, which is that there is ultimately a desire to connect—a real need to connect."

Which brings us to the crux of this story: Baitz created *Brothers & Sisters* with the idea of telling a certain kind of story, about a matriarch, about her children, about political dialogue in this country—"all of the things that I believed would have made a great television show." The network's ambitions were baser. When their vision and Baitz's conflicted, they found their own opinions more compelling. The writers' strike occurred allowing the abrogation of writers' contracts. Baitz vented, in public, in blog posts. The network went ahead without him, producing four more years of episodes.

Baitz took all of this hard. He withdrew to eastern Long Island to write a play. It was as if, he said, he had to teach himself to write again. "I worked hard, and I got it again...You have to really dedicate yourself to doing this work."

Other Desert Cities was born from that abyss. "I couldn't have written this play without the *Brothers & Sisters* experience, and the rants and the rage," Baitz said. He explains: "I guess [I've come] to really understand balance, the nature of balance. and also I've really come to understand the danger of a writer's presuppositions and the lack of humility about a subject."

Although Baitz grew up in a Beverly Hills house once owned by the manager of Grauman's Chinese, "steeped in the ethnographic understanding of what LA means and show business," he now feels grateful for the experience of *Brothers & Sisters,* "while incredibly painful and incredibly expensive in both the literal sense and the emotional sense, it saved me. It was the right thing to do. I still have a relationship to Hollywood. It's just that I don't need to have a relationship to Hollywood." (He has, however, recently sold another TV project to Hollywood).

Baitz now finds himself back in Los Angeles with this play, imbued with greater self-knowledge and a clearer mission in his work. "The first part of my life was spent in great confusion. By the time I reached age 40, 10 years ago, that confusion had turned into misery; and since then I've tried very, very hard to find reason, pride and connectivity in art, in literature, in love, in nature, and so connect."

Just as the play's title refers to a highway exit sign, offering alternatives beyond Palm Springs, so, too, Baitz's play seeks an alternative way out of the seeming impasses of our times—our political deadlocks, our family dramas, even our most heartfelt and ego-driven certitudes—by making us experience a greater emotional truth. In *Other Desert Cities,* we may not find that which unites us, but, instead, be gobsmacked by the realization that our most deeply held beliefs about the people we know best are, like a proverbial desert mirage, not exactly as they seem.

Baitz's affirmation may be as simple as believing, to quote *The X-Files,* that "the truth is out there."

November 21. 2012

VISUALIZING JEWISH VOICES

Here's a challenge: Let's say you had $1.1 million to give away on a program to inspire people working in Jewish organizations as well as the people who find themselves in their public spaces.

What would you do? Hand out baseball cards with the pictures of famous rabbis and leaders? Produce mix tapes of Israeli rap music?

Philanthropist Harold Grinspoon had a different idea, and the result can be seen in an exhibition at the Skirball Cultural Center of eighteen posters commissioned to marry the work of great Jewish graphic designers and artists with inspirational Jewish quotes. Called *Voices & Visions,* the display is on view through March 17.

The featured quotes range from Martin Buber ("All journeys have secret destinations of which the traveler is unaware") to the Baal Shem Tov ("From every human being there rises a light"). There are rabbis galore: Hillel, Tarfon, Akiva, Heschel as well as authors such as Blu Greenberg and Susan Sontag.

My personal favorite is designed by Paula Scher. All it shows is a person purposefully walking, wearing a suit, depicted in profile from the waist down, with a quote from Rabbi

Abraham Joshua Heschel: "When I marched in Selma, I felt my legs were praying."

There is also a series of accompanying texts—viewable online at skirball.org—that are produced by writers as diverse as Erica Brown, Rabbi Daniel Gordis, Rabbi Joseph Telushkin and Rabbi Irving Greenberg.

Grinspoon's eponymous foundation, located in western Massachusetts, recently distributed 6,000 complete sets of the posters to Jewish institutions, PJ Library partners and cultural organizations. They are available for free through the program (voices-visions.org), at least for the first set, and there is a limited, signed edition that either will be given, offered for sale or offered at auction.

The concept behind the project is the famous ad campaign by the Container Corp. of America, called *Great Ideas of Western Man,* which ran between 1950 and 1975. Its posters by accomplished artists and designers such as Fernand Léger, Milton Glaser and Saul Bass, featured quotes from such inspirational thinkers as John Stuart Mill, Woodrow Wilson and Abraham Lincoln.

Grinspoon wondered if the same could be done pairing great Jewish quotes with Jewish graphic designers and artists. He discussed the idea with his friend Nancy Berman, a former curator of the Jewish Museum in New York and the founding director emerita of the Skirball. Berman knew Louis Danziger, who had worked on the original Container Corp. campaign. He, in turn, suggested Arnold Schwartzman as artistic director, at which point the project began to take shape.

Schwartzman was born in London, and, as a child during World War II, his home was destroyed on the first day of the

Blitz—his family had to be dug out of the rubble. Later, his family ran a kosher hotel in the seaside resort of Margate. He attended art school and then went into military service and was posted to the Korean DMZ, where his chaplain was Chaim Potok, the author and rabbi. Upon his return, he began a career as a graphic designer, first in television and then in advertising.

Schwartzman, who moved to Los Angeles in 1978, has brought his talent to everything from the *London Times* to Coca-Cola commercials to the 1984 Olympic Games, where he was design director. He won an Oscar for best documentary feature for 1981's *Genocide,* has consulted on design to the Academy Awards since 1996 and has produced some 10 books, numerous films and too many ads to tally. In 2002, Queen Elizabeth appointed him Officer of the Most Excellent Order of the British Empire.

Schwartzman has been a longtime member of the prestigious Alliance Graphique Internationale, an organization of the world's greatest graphic designers, and the friendships he developed there informed the all-star list of graphic designers and artists he assembled for *Voices & Visions*: Glaser and George Tscherny (both of whom worked on the original Container Corp. campaign), Art Paul (Playboy's founding art director, who came up with the bunny logo), Hungarian-born Israeli design icon Dan Reisinger, R. O. Blechman (known widely for his New Yorker cartoons), Israeli master designer Yarom Vardimon and many others, including Schwartzman himself.

All are Jewish, for which Schwartzman has no explanation other than the pattern of Jews entering professions for which there was no bar to entry; those raised in religious homes who rebelled by finding a vocation making graven images; and a realization that the grandchildren and great-grandchildren of peddlers, once ensconced in advertising and "brand identity," remained good salesmen. The styles are eclectic, from typography-dominated to visual symbols, from the fine art to the abstractly commercial, some in which Jewish references exist subtly and others more obviously.

Voices & Visions was supposed to take four months to put together; instead, it took eighteen months. Madeline Calabrese, the program director, explained that a "quote team" was created that not only researched and found potential quotes to be used, but also cleared them, when necessary, for copyright purposes. This took some time.

The purpose of the posters, Calabrese said, is to beautify space in Jewish public institutions as well as render old quotes anew, to "let the artist develop a first take" and trust that conversations will ensue.

The notion that a poster can change a mind, brighten a day or start a conversation seems at first far-fetched. But as people read less, the way they connect to thoughts and information is increasingly graphic and design-driven. (There's a reason Apple Inc. is worth as much as it is).

At the Skirball, there is a companion exhibit, *Decades of Dissent,* which features posters that effectively politicized the world. Meanwhile, at the Hammer Museum, there is an exhibit, *Graphic Design: Now in Production,* on logo and brand identity design as well as book design and infographics.

All of which reminds us that although a picture may be worth a thousand words, great design helps us see those words in new ways and find new meaning in sayings that have themselves stood the test of time.

December 20, 2012

THE MASTER DESIGNER: ARNOLD SCHWARTZMAN

Arnold Schwartzman, the artistic director of the *Voices & Visions* program and one of the most accomplished designers and documentary directors of our times, is a story unto himself. Recently, I spent a few very companionable hours at Schwartzman's LA home as he shared some of the details of his personal journey and professional career.

As Schwartzman related, he was born in modest circumstances in London's East End. His mother was born in England, and his father had arrived as a young child from Lodz, Poland. His father worked as head waiter at London's Savoy Hotel. However, during World War II on the first day of the Blitz, their home was bombed. "We actually had to be dug out of the rubble," Schwartzman recalled. His parents survived, but he was evacuated to the countryside for the duration of the war.

After the war, his parents moved to Margate, a seaside resort that had been evacuated during the war. Seizing the opportunity, they started a rooming house, which in turn they traded up to purchase and run a small kosher hotel. (Coincidentally, it had been used at one point during the war to house the children of the Kindertransport.) Schwartzman is currently at work on a documentary about Margate.

Recalling his war-interrupted childhood, Schwartzman said, "I had an almost nonexistent formal education. I taught myself to read and write. What I liked was to draw. My parents didn't know what to do with me. They wanted me to go into the hotel business. I wanted to draw. So I went to art school."

Military service followed. Schwartzman was posted to the DMZ in Korea, where his chaplain was Rabbi (and later author) Chaim Potok. Many years later, Schwartzman asked Potok to write the introduction to his book, *Graven Images.*

After military service, Schwartzman found work as a graphic designer, first in television, then in advertising as a creative director. "My major account was Coca-Cola," Schwartzman said, recalling that, "I got the Who to perform for our commercials." From advertising he became design director for Terence Conran's company, but managing people didn't appeal to him so he went off on his own.

A friendship with famed Hollywood graphic designer Saul Bass, who was in London at the time working on his own feature film, *Phase IV,* led to Bass calling him to say: "How about you come to LA to be my design director." Schwartzman demurred but Bass was so enthusiastic and insistent that Schwartzman finally agreed. Within three months, he and Isolde, his second wife (who is also his production partner and manages all the logistics of his projects), had moved to Los Angeles—this was 1978—and they've been here ever since.

Schwartzman liked Los Angeles, but working for Bass? Not so much. "Once again, it was a mistake. I was running a studio, managing lots of people but not doing as much design." After six months he resigned. Bass took him out for a drink, and asked: "What are you going to do now?" Bass told him that just that morning he'd got a call from this new organization, the Simon Wiesenthal Center, to do a fifteen-minute film for them. Bass had imagined they might do it together but as Schwartzman had quit, he'd turned them down. A few minutes later, Bass said, "You're not doing anything now, why don't you do it?" That was the start of *Genocide.*

What began as a short ftfeen-minute film for the nascent museum took more than two years and involved research in archives in West Germany, France and at Yad Vashem in Israel. While in Jerusalem, Schwartzman was able to contact British historian Martin Gilbert, who also happened to be there. "Within months he wrote a fantastic script." The Wiesenthal Center was able to get Elizabeth Taylor and Orson Welles to narrate. Schwartzman was able to get Elmer Bernstein to do the score.

They originally conceived of having multi-projectors telling the story—eventually 21 in all, coordinated by computers. When they finally screened the film, the response was so favorable that one of the viewers, Barry Manilow, suggested that if they put it together as being disseminated from one projector, then it could be submitted for the Oscars, which they did just in time—and won the best documentary feature Oscar for 1982.

Schwartzman also regaled me with an anecdote about Simon Wiesenthal, whom he got to know during the making of *Genocide.* Once when visiting Wiesenthal's overstuffed office in Vienna, Schwartzman spied a card file bursting out of cabinet, marked "M." Is that for Mengele? Schwartzman asked. "No," Wiesenthal explained, "It's for 'Meshugges.' You wouldn't believe some of the letters I get!"

Schwartzman consulted on several more films for the Wiesenthal Center over the years, including *Echoes That Remain* (1991) and *Liberation*(1994).

Another incipient organization, the Skirball, asked Schwartzman to consult on the graphic design of their initial installation, which included Jewish timeline panels as well as a kaleidoscope room of Jewish images."That was fun putting that together." Since then, Schwartzman has also consulted on other exhibits for the Museum of Tolerance.

Since 1996, he has designed many key elements of the Academy Awards, including posters, trailers and programs both for the award ceremony as well as the Governor's Ball. In 2010, the Cunard Line commissioned Schwartzman to paint two murals for their new "Queen Elizabeth" ocean liner.

Which brings us back to *Voices & Visions* exhibit. What was supposed to take four months, took 18. A lucky number in Jewish lore. Lucky, I would say, for *Voices & Visions*—for Schwartzman proved to be not just a master designer for the poster initiative but also a master among designers.

December 21, 2012

ALSO BY TOM TEICHOLZ

Greetings from Tommywood, (Volume One). Pondwood Press, 2015.
Son of Tommywood, (Volume Two). Pondwood Press, 2015.
Tommywood III: The Column Strikes Back! (Volume Three). Pondwood Press, 2015.
Tommywood Jr., Jr.: The Gospel According to Tommywood (Volume Four). Pondwood Press, 2015.
Close Encounters of the Tommywood Kind (Volume Six). Pondwood Press, 2015.
Wilshire Boulevard Temple and the Warner Murals: Celebrating 150 Years by Tom Teicholz, Oro Editions, San Francisco, CA 2014.
The Jewish Role in American Life, Casden Insitute Annual Study, Volume 1, by Barry Glassner, Hillary Lachner, and Tom Teicholz, USC / Casden Institute, Los Angeles, CA, 2008.
Like No Other Store: Bloomingdale's and the Revolution in American Marketing by Marvin Traub and Tom Teicholz, Times Books/Random House, New York, New York, 1993.
The Trial of Ivan The Terrible: State of Israel vs. John Demjanjuk by Tom Teicholz, St.Martin's Press, New York, New York, 1990.
Conversations with Jerzy Kosinski, edited and with an introduction by Tom Teicholz, University Press of Mississippi, Jackson, Mississippi, 1993.

Conversations with S. J. Perelman, edited and with an introduction by Tom Teicholz, University Press of Mississippi, Jackson, Mississippi, 1995.

Other books and anthologies containing Tom Teicholz's work:

Encyclopedia Judaica, Second Edition. Tom Teicholz, American Film and TV editor., 2006.

Conversations with Isaac Bashevis Singer, University Press of Mississippi, Jackson, Mississippi, 1992.

Writers at Work, Volume 8, The Paris Review Interviews, Viking/Penguin, New York, 1988.

ACKNOWLEDGEMENTS

I am grateful to The Jewish Journal where this work originally appeared in print; and to the editors, proofreaders, and designers who made my work more readable; and to The Huffington Post for allowing me to repost my work there.

I also want to thank the contributors to The TOMMYWOOD Collection IndieGogo campaign for their support and generosity which made publication possible, most notably my tzadiks, hoochems and benefactors: Sandy Climan, Bracken Darrell, Lawrence Schoen, Toni and John Schulman, Bob & Cori Davenport, Peter Graham and Heidi Drymer, Ken & Teri Hertz, Wally & Helen Weiss, Dede Arnholz, Chuck Leavitt, Sharon Nazarian, Chris Pilkington, Stacy and Massimo Pinello, Robert & Edie Parker, Annie Scichili, and Richard Wolloch.

There is more to a book than just writing its content. You need talented people to successfully prepare it for publication. The reason this book looks so terrific is because of designer Devin Tanchum and the very talented folks at Rare Bird Lit, notably my book guru Tyson Cornell and his excellent associates Alice Elmer and Violet Sarosi, as well as Winona Leon (who did the design work for my IndieGogo Campaign). I also want to thank John Vaskis and John Trigonis at IndieGogo for teaching me so much about crowdfunding and helping make this book possible.

ABOUT THE AUTHOR

Tom Teicholz is an award-winning journalist, producer, and content consultant who has created print, video, and social media content for Intel, Logitech, The Museum of Tolerance, and The Milken Family Foundation as well as for several not-for-profits and private clients. His work has appeared in *The New York Times* Sunday magazine, *The Los Angeles Review of Books*, *The Los Angeles Times* Op-Ed page, Newsweek.com, *The Paris Review*, *The New Yorker's 'Talk of the Town'*, *Narrative Magazine*, Forbes.com and the *Huffington Post.* He lives with his wife and daughter in Santa Monica, CA.

www.ingramcontent.com/pod-product-compliance
Lightning Source LLC
Chambersburg PA
CBHW020627110726
47899CB00002B/677

* 9 7 8 0 9 8 8 3 9 6 4 9 4 *